Counterinsurgency Leadership
in Afghanistan, Iraq, and Beyond

Edited by
Nicholas J. Schlosser and James M. Caiella

Marine Corps University Press
Quantico, Virginia

Contents

Foreword

by Major General Robert B. Neller, USMC

This volume collects the works presented at the 2009 symposium "Counterinsurgency Leadership in Afghanistan, Iraq, and Beyond." This one-day colloquium was cohosted by the Marine Corps University and the Marine Corps University Foundation and held at the National Press Club in Washington, DC.

Our recent experiences in Afghanistan and Iraq have shown once again the difference that excellent leadership can make in irregular warfare. Thrust unexpectedly into counterinsurgency situations in 2002 and 2003, American commanders had to operate under difficult and constantly changing conditions. Some adapted quickly; others adjusted over a longer period of time with the help of experience and education. Selecting the right commanders became more important than ever to unit effectiveness. We have come a long way in recent years, but opportunities for further improvement in leadership development and command selection remain.

The leaders of our Afghan and Iraqi allies have also played vital roles in combating the insurgents. Indigenous and host-nation forces enjoy natural advantages in dealing with the population, and provide badly needed manpower in areas where foreign troops are too few and cannot remain indefinitely. With a thorough understanding of our allies and local political and social conditions, we can help newborn nations develop the leadership required for long-term success.

The need for leadership goes beyond today's conflicts and, indeed, lies at the heart of current debates over the future of our national security organizations and strategy. Although most of the public discourse thus far has concentrated on questions of equipment and future threats, leadership will also be a crucial variable. As national security professionals, we must strive to ensure that the nation fields the leaders best suited to tackling the challenges of the twenty-first century.

Robert B. Neller
Major General, U.S. Marine Corps
President, Marine Corps University

Introduction

Counterinsurgency Leadership in Afghanistan, Iraq, and Beyond

by Nicholas J. Schlosser

In a 2009 speech, General David H. Petraeus related how, during his time as the commander of Multi National Force–Iraq, he encountered a sign on a company commander's door that read, "In the absence of orders or guidance, figure out what they should have been and execute vigorously."[1] This quotation synthesizes two fundamental tenets of effective leadership in a counterinsurgency. First, there is the imperative for commanders to impart a clear intent and vision to their subordinates that will enable them to "figure out" the best and most effective means for battling the insurgency. Second, there is a need for subordinate commanders to innovate, adapt, and implement effective counterinsurgency (COIN) tactics on their own initiative.

---

[1] Gen David H. Petraeus, USA, "Commander's remarks, Center for a New American Security, June 11, 2009," http://www.centcom.mil/from-the-commander/commanders-remarks-center-for-a-new-american-security-june-11-2009, (accessed July 15, 2010).

The following selections illustrate how these two factors have formed the foundation for effective COIN leadership. The wars in Iraq and Afghanistan have brought a renewed interest in COIN warfare. In both of these conflicts, U.S. forces have found themselves in a constantly changing battlefield environment, frequently with little in terms of specific guidance regarding tactics and strategy. As a result, the leadership abilities of individual Marines, soldiers, sailors, and airmen—ranging from the commanders of fire teams and squads to the commanders of Marine expeditionary forces and Army corps—often became a decisive factor in the success or failure of a particular operation.

This volume—based on the proceedings of Marine Corps University's "Counterinsurgency Leadership in Afghanistan, Iraq, and Beyond" symposium held in Washington, DC, in September 2009—contains the thoughts, arguments, experiences, and observations of twenty scholars, soldiers, Marines, and policy makers. This collection presents an exploration of COIN leadership in all of its facets and includes chapters on the roles that civilian leadership, military leadership, civil-military cooperation, advisory operations, and alliance relations play in confronting and defeating insurgencies.

Among the variety of perspectives, some salient themes and arguments underpin the entries in this volume and provide a number of basic assertions regarding COIN leadership. First, there are the unique qualities of effective COIN leaders. The second theme is the role civil-military relationships and alliances play in counterinsurgencies. The third is the importance of commanders to the success of COIN operations.

The first is the assertion that COIN leadership requires a unique set of skills that set it apart from leadership in irregular warfare. As Nathaniel C. Fick points out in his chapter, the traits needed for effective COIN leadership are nearly identical to the fourteen Marine Corps leadership traits.[2] As Mark Moyar and Eliot A. Cohen note, however, COIN leadership requires a specific set of characteristics and traits distinct from other forms of combat leadership. Moyar's chapter explores the impact effective and ineffective civilian and military leaders can have upon a successful counterinsurgency operation.[3] In the course of his piece, Moyar

---

[2] Nathaniel C. Fick, chapter 7, "Officer Development for Counterinsurgency."

[3] Mark Moyar, chapter 1, "Counterinsurgency Leadership: The Key to Afghanistan and Iraq."

further makes the argument that while commanders skilled at COIN operations also have the traits and skills necessary for conducting regular warfare operations, the opposite is not necessarily true.

Cohen's chapter makes similar contentions regarding the uniqueness of COIN leadership.[4] He focuses on the challenges facing civil authorities in both the United States and host nations, and outlines a range of unique challenges facing commanders-in-chief during counterinsurgencies that include finding generals with the specific characteristics best suited for this type of warfare, avoiding a heavy reliance on metrics such as elections and territory gained to measure success, integrating civil and military command at the local level, and practicing strategic patience. Cohen also reminds readers of another challenge facing COIN leaders: the need for cooperation between the outside power and the host nation. As he points out, while the United States may perceive counterinsurgencies as small, limited wars, they are total wars for the host nation, upon which the country's very survival hangs.

This asymmetrical dynamic grants considerable bargaining power to the host nation's leaders. Consequently, the importance of alliance relationships and need for close cooperation between diplomats, advisors, and military commanders is a second theme that runs through this volume. The panel discussion among Robert D. Kaplan, Clare Lockhart, Amin Tarzi, and Jeffrey Gedmin is a timely reminder that success or failure in defeating an insurgency hinges on whether the host nation's government enjoys legitimacy in the eyes of its people.[5] The panelists, speaking not long after the controversial and disputed 2009 Afghan elections, provide insight and perspective on the dynamics of the Afghan political system. In the course of their discussion, the participants refute the general impression that Afghanistan has been a perennially lawless, chaotic state. As Tarzi and Kaplan observe, the state once had a moderately stable government that was able to ensure security within its borders. Placing the current situation in Afghanistan in perspective, the discussants consider the means needed to restore security and stability to the troubled state.

Expanding on the importance of building alliance relationships in counterinsurgencies is General Petraeus's open discussion with the symposium's

---

[4] Eliot A. Cohen, chapter 2, "Supreme Command in Irregular Warfare."
[5] Robert D. Kaplan, Clare Lockhart, Amin Tarzi, and Jeffrey Gedmin, chapter 12, "The Afghan Election and the Future of Afghanistan's Leadership: A Discussion."

participants. As he points out in Chapter 13, the U.S. forces in Afghanistan are part of a larger, international coalition.[6] Furthermore, U.S. Forces Central Command can only pursue its missions with the help and support of governments in its area of responsibility, a region that stretches from the Red Sea to central Asia. Throughout his discussion, Petraeus stresses that success in Afghanistan is only possible if the North Atlantic Treaty Organization (NATO) can build strong partnerships with both the host nation as well as bordering states such as Pakistan. As he notes about Pakistan, "Countering terrorism requires more than counterterrorist forces, it requires a whole-of-governments counterinsurgency mindset. It does not mean that those forces have to be yours. And I think Pakistan is a great example of that. There, the Pakistanis are doing the fighting for which we are providing substantial assistance."[7]

The chapters by Colonel Jeffery M. Haynes and retired Lieutenant General David W. Barno provide further insight into the character of the conflict in Afghanistan. Chapter 10 by Barno and retired Colonel John K. Wood presents an overview of the current situation in Afghanistan and lays out the challenges facing NATO as it strives to build a stable, legitimate Afghan state.[8] The authors propose a range of strategies, including rebuilding civil-military relationships and reframing the public narrative. Meanwhile, Haynes's chapter describes the techniques and procedures used to build and advise Afghanistan's military force, drawing on his own experience as an adviser to the Afghan National Army's 201st Corps.[9]

The third and final theme running through this work is the critical importance commanders in the field have in shaping the character of overall COIN strategy. The chapters by Brigadier General H. R. McMaster, Brigadier General W. Blake Crowe, and retired Colonel Peter R. Mansoor provide insight and recommendations into how regimental and brigade commanders can best utilize the combat and logistical resources of their formations to conduct effective COIN operations.[10] A brigade's

---

[6] Chapter 13, "A Conversation with General David H. Petraeus."

[7] Ibid.

[8] LtGen David W. Barno, USA (Ret), and Col John K. Wood, USA (Ret), chapter 10, "Winning in Afghanistan."

[9] Col Jeffery M. Haynes, USMC, chapter 11, "Advising Afghan Military Forces."

[10] BGen H. R. McMaster, USA, chapter 3, "The Art of Brigade Command in Counterinsurgency,"; Col Peter R. Mansoor, USA (Ret), chapter 4, "Brigade Command in Counterinsurgency Operations: Lessons from the Iraq War,"; BGen W. Blake Crowe, USMC, chapter 5, "Regimental Command in Counterinsurgency."

and regiment's tasks include defeating insurgent fighters in the field, establishing security, and laying the foundations for stability. As Crowe's chapter illustrates, this sometimes forces regiments to provide local governance as well as administration. As he notes in referring to his service as a regimental commander in western Iraq, "In 2006, we were the surrogate government. We did not have mayors at the time. The provincial governor was in Ramadi and he stayed there."[11]

As the selection by McMaster demonstrates, however, the most important formations in counterinsurgencies are usually smaller than regiments and brigades. As he reminds readers, "I think it's important for us to understand that success in these wars really depends on effective operations at much lower levels, such as at the platoon, company, and battalion levels."[12] Chapter 6 highlights the importance of battalion level forces in COIN operations. In this panel discussion, Francis J. "Bing" West, Colonel David J. Furness, Colonel William M. Jurney, and Colonel Julian Dale Alford describe how battalion commanders have prepared and trained their companies to best battle insurgent forces and defend and win over the local populace.[13] Drawing on their own experiences in Iraq and Afghanistan, Furness, Jurney, and Alford all highlight how initiative, adaptability, and creativity are essential factors for successful COIN leaders. They also remind readers how the scattered, unpredictable, and clandestine nature of insurgent strategies forces all officers, whether they are corps commanders or platoon commanders, to understand the impact their actions can have upon the entire campaign. Most important, they highlight the need for inventiveness and resourcefulness in the field.

How to produce competent and skilled officers for COIN operations is the subject of the chapters by Thomas E. Ricks, Nathaniel Fick, and Paula D. Broadwell. As Ricks notes in Chapter 9, "I think there's no accident…that the first effective, sustained COIN campaigns in Iraq took place very far from Baghdad."[14] Paula Broadwell reinforces and expands on this assertion when she reminds readers that "COIN and full spectrum operations require that we invest great authority, responsibility, and resources

---

[11] Crowe, "Regimental Command in Counterinsurgency."

[12] McMaster, "Brigade Command in Counterinsurgency."

[13] Hon. Francis J. "Bing" West; Col David J. Furness, USMC; Col William M. Jurney, USMC; and Col Julian Dale Alford, USMC, chapter 6, "The Art of Battalion Command in Counterinsurgency: A Discussion."

[14] Thomas E. Ricks, chapter 9, "Generalship and Counterinsurgency."

at the lowest operational ranks."[15] Both these chapters, as well as the contribution by Fick, outline the problems and challenges facing the U.S. military as it builds an adaptive, versatile, and competent officer corps capable of fighting future conflicts, many, if not most, of which will be small wars akin to those in Iraq and Afghanistan. Ricks argues that the reluctance to use relief as a tool of command has severely weakened the general officer corps of the U.S. Army. Meanwhile, Broadwell and Fick illustrate the process of developing effective junior officers for the future, with Broadwell looking at institutional developments and challenges and Fick providing a personal account of his service as a lieutenant in the Marine Corps.

In sum, this volume gives readers a diverse collection of perspectives, insights, and recommendations for COIN and war fighting in the 21st century. The breadth of the topics discussed is a testament to how crucial effective governance, cultural understanding, civil affairs, and military operations are to COIN. Furthermore, the collection demonstrates how competent leaders are necessary to bring these often disparate elements together into a cohesive whole and a multifaceted campaign that can effectively defeat insurgencies on the military, political, cultural, and economic battlefields. With international terrorism and global insurgency remaining a persistent threat, an exploration of this subject remains timely, relevant, and necessary.

*　　*　　*

Dr. Mark Moyar and Major Andrew D. Hamilton organized the conference on which this book is based and initiated the book concept. At Marine Corps University Press, Senior Editor Kenneth H. Williams and editors Shawn H. Vreeland and Wanda J. Renfrow provided editorial guidance and helped to adapt the papers and presentations for publication. Marine Corps History Division intern Max von Bargen also provided editorial support. The book was designed by Vincent J. Martinez.

Dr. Nicholas J. Schlosser
Marine Corps History Division

---

[15] Paula D. Broadwell, chapter 8, "The 'Major' Challenge of Junior Officer Leadership Development and Talent Management."

Part I
Counterinsurgency Leadership

Chapter 1

Counterinsurgency Leadership: The Key to Afghanistan and Iraq

by Mark Moyar

Counterinsurgency (COIN) leadership is an incredibly timely subject, especially since our government's top leaders are now considering a new strategy for Afghanistan that has everything to do with COIN leadership. It is also a timeless subject. Commanders who succeeded at COIN in the campaigns of Alexander the Great or the American Civil War were similar in most respects to the commanders who have succeeded in Afghanistan and Iraq during our present century. In my view, leadership is and always has been the most important factor in COIN, for it is central to the most important activities of COIN—security and governance.

The security side—which consists primarily of securing the population and attacking the insurgents—demands leaders at the local level have the attributes to obtain intelligence from scared civilians, to sustain morale when troops die, and to hunt the enemy relentlessly through cities or jungles.

Above all, the quality of governance hinges on the integrity and competence of leaders. Poor leadership is the root cause of all the Afghan government's dire problems cited in Army General Stanley A. McChrystal's new report—from the failure to protect the people to corruption to the absence of justice.

Not all of the experts gathered here today would agree that leadership quality stands at the pinnacle of COIN. The adherents of the "hearts and minds" school, for example, assign higher priority to remediating social and economic grievances. But I don't believe that any will contend that leadership is unimportant. Our agreement on the importance of command gives us all an interest in working to improve leadership quality, which is our principal objective today.

I also believe that how we prioritize leadership quality will greatly affect our ability to change it. If it doesn't stand near the top of the priority list, it won't receive adequate resources or command attention. Too often counterinsurgents have concentrated so intently on which methods should be used that they neglect the more important question of who should use those methods. Many counterinsurgencies have, in fact, been run aground by relegating leadership to a secondary concern. The beginnings of the wars in Afghanistan and Iraq are two unhappy examples. In Iraq, after the fall of Saddam Hussein, the head of the Coalition Provisional Authority, L. Paul Bremer, dismantled the Iraqi regime and barred its leaders from governmental service in the belief that the old elites could be easily replaced by new ones, and he could therefore focus his attention on methods and resources. Bremer gave government leadership positions to Iraqi exiles whose good manners and Western educations gave them a veneer of skill that masked their real dearth of experience and talent.

When the United States pressed the baton into the hand of Iyad Allawi's interim Iraqi government in June 2004, it granted the Iraqis full authority over leadership appointments. Multi National Force–Iraq (MNF-I) commanding General George W. Casey Jr. and others in the U.S. military were soon citing this decision as a colossal error, and with good reason. Personal, political, and sectarian connections took precedence over merit in Iraqi personnel decisions. When Iraqi governmental security forces and administrators were brought in to hold areas after Americans forces had cleared them, they often could not prevent the insurgents from returning, primarily because their officers were not experienced or committed enough to organize effective resistance to enemy attacks.

In Afghanistan, the United States and its North Atlantic Treaty Organization (NATO) allies at first entrusted the organs of government to regional warlords who were, almost to a man, inclined toward corruption and human rights violations. From the early stages of the war, the warlords dominated the leadership of the police, the most troublesome part of the Afghan government. President Hamid Karzai exacerbated matters by handing commands in the security forces to friends, relatives, and political supporters of unsavory character. With regrettable regularity, poorly led police have indulged in extortion, kidnapping, and all the other abuses listed in General McChrystal's report, which together have turned the Pashtun belt into fertile soil for insurgent recruiters. And the police's appetite for abusing the populace has too infrequently been accompanied by an appetite for abusing the insurgents.

The good news is that most counterinsurgencies have several levers available that can sharply improve the quality of their leaders. History shows that the most effective levers are to be found in one of four broad categories: leader development, command selection, co-option of elites, and delegation of authority.

There are a few examples from recent events in Iraq and Afghanistan that provide evidence of the potential for improvement. The remarkable Sunni Awakening from 2005 to 2007 reversed the tide of war in Iraq's Sunni areas primarily by co-opting talented and experienced Sunni elites. It was made possible by an American policy shift that authorized tribal engagement, but it also required the exertions of excellent American field commanders who led the unrelenting military operations, oversaw the basic governance, and conducted the protracted tea-table negotiations required to convince fence-sitting sheikhs to move their tribes to the American side.

The 2007 surge owed much of its success to improvements in Iraqi command selection and to co-option of additional Iraqi elites. Over the course of the year, with the Americans cajoling and at times threatening to withdraw aid, the Iraqi government relieved army commanders as high as division level, along with seven of the nine National Police brigade commanders and more than 2,000 Iraqi Interior Ministry personnel. As a consequence, the Iraqi security forces started killing insurgents and stopped filling the streets and sewers with the bodies of civilians who belonged to the wrong Muslim denomination. In addition, General David H. Petraeus,

General Casey's successor as the commander of MNF-I, increased the overall quality of the leadership committed to population security by assigning more American forces to that mission. More elites came over to the government's side because of counterinsurgent military success and continuing tribal engagement.

In Afghanistan, serious efforts in leader development and command selection have originated with a few cabinet officials. Defense Minister Abdul Rahim Wardak has achieved major progress in both areas over the past five years, which has done much to make the Afghan National Army the most effective and impartial of Afghanistan's institutions. The Afghan Interior Ministry did not have a high-caliber leader at the helm until the appointment of Mohammad Hanif Atmar in fall 2008. Since taking office, Atmar has replaced corrupt police chiefs with better men and invigorated the ministry, with considerable help from the United States, which wisely ramped up support to the ministry in 2008. He is, nevertheless, limited in what he can accomplish in the short-term by the shortage of experienced Afghan police officers and the ongoing influence of the warlords. Whether Afghanistan's president retains the senior leadership in the defense and interior ministries after the election is resolved, or replaces them for political or personal reasons, it could reshape the future of Afghanistan's COIN leadership.

The rates of Afghan force expansion could also fundamentally alter the leadership dynamics. Rapid doubling or tripling of the host-nation security forces, which many in Washington and some in Kabul now recommend, has failed in countless other counterinsurgencies for the same basic reason—insufficient leadership. New forces can be created in six months by putting men in uniform and administering rudimentary training, but forging the battalion commanders to lead them takes ten or twenty years. In the absence of seasoned leaders, troops crack under fire. They will steal people's chickens, goats, or whatever other delectable farm animals they can lay their fingers on. Many will desert and some will go over to the enemy, taking their weapons with them, which happened repeatedly in Afghanistan during the 1980s when the Soviets fielded ill-led Afghan COIN forces.

If top U.S. leaders decide on a dramatic expansion of the Afghan security forces in the next few years, certain measures can be taken to prevent those disastrous consequences, albeit at significant cost. In my estimation, assuring quality will require either the very large step of placing Afghan forces under the command of the NATO officers who are leading their partner units, or else the deployment of many additional NATO personnel as advisers or members of partner units. In other words, without that very large step, we cannot use expansion of the Afghan security forces as a substitute for foreign troop increases. Afghan and NATO forces, and particularly American forces, will have to increase in number together. I also think it is worthwhile to debate whether advising or partnering is more helpful to the Afghan security forces.

While host-nation leadership has been and remains the most important problem in both Iraq and Afghanistan, American COIN leadership has had its imperfections as well. American commanders do not regularly commit basic errors that have been common among Iraqi and Afghan officers, such as doing nothing all day, fleeing in panic at the first glimpse of a hostile weapon, or demanding bribes from civilians at roadside checkpoints. Nevertheless, some have been much more effective as leaders than others because of differences in key attributes.

The more creative and flexible commanders have improvised effectively and devised new methods adapted to local conditions, while others have not. Some have shown greater initiative than others in military operations or intelligence collection or civil affairs. Success in building relationships with key local power players has varied widely from one place to another according to the social skills and competence of the American commander on the scene.

The ranges of variation in these attributes have been wider in the Army than in the Marine Corps, and wider still in the National Guard and Reserves. From the early experiences in Iraq, senior Army generals recognized an insufficiency in creativity and flexibility among certain officers and took effective remedial measures, from training and education to promotion and command selection. A number of Army generals also concluded that risk-aversion within the service was impeding initiative, and they sought to promote risk-taking, although those reform efforts appear to have been less fruitful thus far. When I surveyed Marine and U.S. Army veterans of Iraq and Afghanistan on COIN topics last year, I found that just 28 percent of Army respondents believed that their service encouraged risk-taking by company and battalion commanders. By contrast, 58 percent of Marine respondents said as much of their service, which provides a good indicator of the room for improvement that remains within the Army.

That survey's results also indicated that both the Marine Corps and the Army have been too tolerant of bad leadership in Afghanistan and Iraq. Fifty-nine percent of the soldiers and 49 percent of the Marines said that American commanders ought to be relieved for poor performance more often. According to the respondents, onerous procedures for relieving commanders have discouraged firings. So have personal sympathy and concern about creating a harmful command climate. It is true that too many firings of commanders is likely to stifle initiative, especially if done carelessly, but I still think we should more often adopt the attitude of Ramon del Fierro Magsaysay, whose large-scale firings in the Philippines during the early 1950s facilitated the defeat of the Huk Rebellion. When a committee of generals complained to Magsaysay that all the personnel changes were demoralizing the army, he replied, "I don't care. If they are bad I will demoralize them some more."

Influential elements inside today's U.S. military worry that focusing heavily on COIN preparedness will leave the United States ill-prepared for conventional warfare. This argument has considerable merit with respect to organization and weapons systems, but I don't believe that it holds true with respect to leadership. Good COIN leaders also tend to be good conventional leaders. Good conventional leaders, on the other hand, have often failed in COIN, because they don't have the extra attributes required of COIN commanders.

This point is most evident in generations of military officers with years of experience in both COIN and conventional warfare, of which the prime American example is the generation that commanded during the Civil War and Reconstruction. Philip H. Sheridan, for instance, emerged from the Civil War's conventional battles as one of the Union's greatest generals, yet became one of the Union's biggest failures in the COIN operations of Reconstruction because he lacked critical attributes of COIN leadership. As the Union's top commander in Texas during Reconstruction, Sheridan did not show the flexibility or ingenuity in administering thorny Reconstruction policies that more successful commanders displayed. He avoided cultivating Texan elites and allowed Federal troops to brutalize the general population in revenge for insurgent depredations because of his poor judgment and contempt for the population, which are best illustrated in his remark to a newspaperman that "if I owned Hell and Texas, I would rent out Texas and live in Hell!"

More than anything else, upcoming decisions on COIN leadership will determine our nation's future COIN capabilities, and hence our ability to protect the nation from the threats posed by insurgents in Afghanistan and other troubled countries. It is our hope that the following chapters will, in some measure, influence the quality of those decisions for the better.

Chapter 2

Supreme Command in Irregular Warfare

by Eliot A. Cohen

What follows reflects a combination of scholarly interest in the problem of supreme command and irregular warfare, and some experience as a practitioner. In the first case, having written a book that dealt with *supreme command*—defined as the civil-military relationship at the very top of the political pyramid—in conventional war, I would like to explore it with regard to unconventional conflict. As for the latter, for two years, from 2007 through the beginning of 2009, I served as counselor of the Department of State, serving as the lead liaison with the deputy national security adviser for Afghanistan and Iraq, traveling extensively to both places, advising Secretary of State Condoleezza Rice with regard to counterinsurgency (COIN), and often representing the department in relevant interagency meetings.

This paper, moreover, focuses on the problem of supreme command in the United States. Associated allies, such as Canada in Afghanistan, face interesting but different challenges. Of course for the host or client country—

Afghanistan or Iraq in the current American case—these are total wars, and in some respects their experience of supreme command will more resemble a conventional conflict because the stakes for which they fight are so great.

Irregular warfare and supreme command in it differ in three important respects from conventional conflict. This is so because, in the first instance, success or failure in irregular warfare has a much more profoundly political character than victory or defeat in conventional war. If you succeed in an irregular war, expect no victory parade, merely a switch to policing, reconciliation, and murky political deals. Outcomes in irregular warfare are blurry; these wars end not with a bang, but with a haggle.

Second, COIN is very much a valley-by-valley war, as a colonel hosting me in Afghanistan once remarked as we flew over his area of responsibility. The macro picture on which statesmen and military commanders rely in conventional war does not really exist in irregular wars. There are no lines moving on a map, no D-Day, no decisive battle. Success in one area may coexist with failure in another, and uncertainty in most.

And third, these are long wars. Assertions that insurgencies last on average ten years are too precise to be convincing, but irregular wars do indeed, by and large, last a long time. They last a lot longer than the wars that generals and politicians alike have studied in university or war colleges.

Six peculiar characteristics of supreme command and COIN come to mind.

First, in irregular warfare, attention at the top is intermittent. For the president and the principals—the secretary of state, secretary of defense, and others of that rank—but even for the larger bureaucracy, irregular warfare is something to which they will devote serious attention, but it does not constitute the first claim on their attention and effort, or does so only sporadically. These leaders face many other claims on their attention and time, and no less important (particularly in the case of the secretary of defense) they must consider the long-term institutional health of their department, much more than they would in the middle of an all out conventional conflict. This divided attention and conflicting interest will breed all kinds of tensions with the theater commander and even the on-the-ground commander.

The second peculiar challenge is the problem of measuring progress. In a big conventional war, you can identify the frontline. You probably have some sense of whether your side is winning or losing—have we taken Guadalcanal or haven't we taken Guadalcanal? Irregular warfare yields no such clarity. The authorities at the top grasp for ways of knowing merely where the trends point, let alone whether they have reached anything like definitive success. In such circumstances, militaries turn to all kinds of metrics, most of them spurious, to measure their success. In a famous essay Bernard Fall, the great Franco-American student of the Vietnam War, described the gap between the French military's measure of success—the areas it controlled in North Vietnam by daylight, and what he took to be the real measure, where the French government could collect taxes. In his view, which proved considerably more accurate than that of the French government, the Vietminh were winning.

As a practical matter, Washington, DC, tends to measure success with three misleading kinds of metrics. The bureaucracy turns first to what it calls *kinetic events* and other kinetic kinds of things—people getting killed, numbers of attacks, and the dramatic quality of those attacks. The intelligence community in particular sometimes forgets that its database exists to support analysis, not supplant it, and violent activity in and of itself does not mean anything more than that a war is going on. A peaceful district may lie completely in the grip of the insurgents, whereas a violent couple of weeks may precede the establishment of government rule in another area—and yet, a kinetically oriented database will record the one as a COIN success, the other as a failure.

Leaders pay a great deal of attention as well to dramatic public events—elections in particular. This was particularly true in the first years in Iraq and Afghanistan, although now some of the charm has worn off. But elections, in particular, may mean less to the local population than provision of basic services, and security above all. Similarly, vote-rigging, influence peddling, and similar political dark arts may not mean a failed COIN, but rather the existence of a political order akin to Chicago in the early twentieth century—corrupt, ugly, and modestly effective.

Finally, the bureaucracy often looks at—and reports up the chain—inputs or measures of effort (dollars spent, civil servants present, projects started), rather than outputs, or what has happened on the ground. It is easy to measure the former, difficult to measure the latter, but do those dollars do any good if they merely divert local doctors and engineers from useful work into higher paying jobs as interpreters, if the aid workers cannot move outside their compound for lack of security, or if the brand new water pump fails in six months because no one has provided for the spare parts and trained technicians to maintain it?

These kinds of metrics appeal to congressmen, political appointees, soldiers, and diplomats alike, and mislead them profoundly. Although some metrics have their uses, there is no definitive set or invariably correct measure. Leaders may simply stumble on them, or use them as crude indications, not precise indicators of what is going on. My own sense that Afghanistan's trends were adverse came from looking at the mobility maps produced by the United Nations (UN) security office in Afghanistan: each year the green areas shrank, the yellow and red (caution and extreme danger, respectively) grew. The trend was unmistakable, even if the particular judgments were questionable. Moreover, as so often in this kind of conflict, the perception mattered as much as the reality: if the maps said, "Don't go here," most aid workers would not go—and that had real consequences.

Nor is it the case that the people in the field, those who are closest to the problem have the best assessments. In this kind of war, intelligence assessments (and this goes for input measures as well) become grades, the grades that people award themselves. From an American point of view, these are wars of a year at a time, and when individuals and units rotate in and out of a war zone they have a tremendous desire to report progress commensurate with their efforts and sacrifices during their tenure.

During my time at the State Department, I repeatedly visited a number of locations in Afghanistan and Iraq. When I visited a unit at the beginning of its rotation, its leaders would invariably report that the situation was much worse than they had been led to believe before they deployed. The mood was one of grim determination against daunting odds. "It's much worse than we thought," the staffs would often say. Six months later, however, they would report cautious optimism: "It's hard going and I won't overpromise, but we think we may have turned the corner here." Visit the same unit at the end of the rotation, and the line was, "We have achieved irreversible momentum." And then the next unit would fall in on the first, and report, once again, grim determination against daunting odds. The issue is not simply one of a learning curve, although that exists, too: it reflects, rather, the can-do spirit running counter to prudent realism.

Reports from the field in such wars get digested and condensed for senior leaders, reducing complex local situations into simple summaries, and becoming even further compressed into short, compelling, and often wildly misleading thumbnail metrics.

The worst example of this that I encountered in government was generated not by the civilians, but by military intelligence and amplified by career bureaucrats in the State Department. It held that 75 percent of the violence in Afghanistan occurred in 10 percent of the districts. The unstated implication, of course, was that the violence in Afghanistan was localized and contained. This statistic appeared often in briefings (including at the very top of the U.S. government), as well as in public testimony. I spent a good two years fighting it, because, after only modest digging, it became apparent how utterly incorrect it was.

The problem began with the utterly false implication that we actually knew what was going on in all the districts of Afghanistan (some 398 of them). We did not, for the simple reason that neither our North Atlantic Treaty Organization (NATO) allies nor the United States had a presence, let alone a substantial presence, in each of those districts. The violence measured most effectively in the so-called SIGACTS (significant acts) database measured violence directed against Americans or violence that Americans initiated against the enemy. Quite apart from some bizarre counting rules (unexploded roadside bombs counted as violent acts), this did not measure the violence directed at Afghans nearly as well, which of course was what counted. And even there, quantitative measures of violence did not account for its political and psychological character. A dozen firefights between American forces and Taliban infiltrators in the mountains meant one thing—the grisly, public execution of an uncooperative tribal elder in front of a terrified village meant something very different, and a lot more from the locals' point of view. Augment those with some nonviolent night letters promising the same for other collaborators with the Americans, and the violence statistics become completely meaningless. But this is what senior leadership in Washington heard, and will often hear.

A third challenge of supreme command in irregular warfare consists of picking the right generals, and clearly this kind of war requires a very particular kind of commander. George S. Patton Jr. probably would not do well waging a COIN. Quite clearly a David H. Petraeus, a Stanley A.

McChrystal, or a James N. Mattis most definitely do. Until they learn the hard way, however, civilians tend to assume that generals are interchangeable commodities, and the military's own promotion systems and norms—particularly those that prescribe a narrow path to high command—reinforce that mistaken impression.

Commanders in these kinds of conflicts require peculiar aptitudes, particularly cultural and political sensitivity, and perhaps less of the large-scale engineering project kind of aptitudes characteristic of large-scale war. Robert M. Gates, a very effective secretary of defense, set a remarkable precedent with his difficult decision to relieve General David D. McKiernan and replace him with General Stanley A. McChrystal. McKiernan, an able conventional commander, had not failed spectacularly, but Gates judged that the situation in Afghanistan required someone with very different skills and background. Gates's decision, however, is remarkable as much for its uniqueness as anything else. By and large, the political level very rarely relieves senior commanders for failure to perform effectively in COIN, and this constitutes a great weakness of the contemporary system of high command.

The integration of the civil-military effort is the fourth challenge of supreme command in irregular warfare. This occurs at the local level, of course, particularly in innovative organizations like the Provincial Reconstruction Teams, and has always occurred in irregular warfare—the Civil Operations and Revolutionary Development Support program in Vietnam being the most successful example. In theory, military people would argue for unity of command, one of those hoary principles of war preached to second lieutenants and colonels alike. In practice, they do not want it. That is, neither they nor their civilian counterparts (ambassadors, for the most part) want the military and civilian side of a COIN to serve under one organization with one boss. It is more convenient, if ultimately debilitating, to have organizations "sticking to their lanes" and coordinating rather than unifying their efforts.

The absence of unity of command bedeviled our efforts in Iraq and, to a lesser extent, in Afghanistan. Instead, American commanders and diplomats proclaimed the merits of unity of effort a second best. To be sure, the relationship between General Petraeus and Ambassador Ryan C. Crocker in Iraq was a marvelous example of just how well this relationship could work. But we should not draw too much from this experience. It required extreme effort, down to the virtual collocation of their offices. It required the qualities of a superb diplomat who could deal effectively not only with fractious Iraqis, but with a brilliant, and very intense, four-star general. Crockers and Petraeuses are rare.

The locus of decision making requires, in itself, a decision. American counterinsurgencies (with the exception of the American Revolution and the Reconstruction) have taken place somewhere else, in the context of a coalition war conducted with and on behalf of a local ally. Americans will wish to decentralize many of our decisions. Our ally, for whom the issues concern political and even personal survival, will wish to centralize theirs. A very good example of this concerns reconciliation of enemy insurgents. We would prefer to leave this to the field; our allies will insist that their central government make the decisions. Given the importance of reconciliation in ending an insurgency, and given the political stakes involved, this is a tug of war the local ally will win.

Between the efficacy of military and civilian organizations there is little to choose. The military will always outrun the civilians in a COIN. It will have vastly greater numbers of people and resources, it will control security, and it will have some skills (planning in particular) that the diplomats and aid professionals will lack. But it is the civilians who will always control the most important account—institution building. There is thus a built-in asymmetry that will be felt in Washington as well as in the field, at the level of the secretary of defense and the secretary of state, but also at the different levels of interagency working groups and in the field.

The fifth challenge for supreme command in irregular warfare is the need for strategic patience. Sometimes in conventional war it is the job of the civilian leadership to push generals to move before they feel ready. Just the reverse often holds true in COIN. That is to say civilian leaders must prepare people to be patient. This means speaking directly and often to their domestic audience, but to the military as well, preparing everyone involved for extended conflict. In COIN, as in all war, raw persistence matters enormously. Often, it dominates intellect. A clever strategy means little if you cannot stick to the course, and many mistakes can be redeemed by dogged willingness to muddle through.

The sixth and final challenge concerns alliance relationships. As noted above, these kinds of wars are about survival for the host government, which gives them an enormous amount of strength in negotiating with a superpower patron. They risk their survival; we do not risk ours. And so in the negotiations that invariably go on at the top level between us and our local ally, they often have the stronger negotiating position.

There are other alliance dimensions to these conflicts. In Iraq and Afghanistan we have sought to conduct coalition COIN and have run into the limits of what can be done. While some of our allies—at the upper end, the British, but also smaller allies such as Denmark—will throw themselves in almost as fully as we will, others will not, handcuffing themselves with all kinds of caveats and self-imposed restraints that can actually create havens for an enemy who knows who is serious about fighting him and who is not. And even the more capable allies may have policy outlooks different from ours, or lack some of the tools that we have. In this case, the arithmetic of alliance does not mean that two U.S. soldiers plus two allied soldiers equals four equally effective counterinsurgent soldiers. In some cases two plus two will equal three, or two, or even fewer. And this is without considering the extraordinarily complicating relationships we have set up with the UN, NATO, and various nongovernmental organizations. One major area that will require study in the aftermath of Iraq and Afghanistan should be a candid appraisal of how much effort we should put into making these coalition exercises, and a realistic appraisal of what the cost for doing so is.

How has the Washington political leadership exercised supreme command? Here we have seen a number of innovations. Secure video teleconferencing between Washington and the theater has had a huge effect, allowing the president to establish a direct personal relationship with his counterpart in Iraq or Afghanistan, as well as with his commanders there. The consequences may be mixed, but technological feasibility usually induces leaders to establish this kind of personal contact. On the whole, and although people in the field would rather hear from Washington by carrier pigeon, it is a good thing. Personal relationships with political counterparts and military subordinates allow a president to act more effectively in a crisis, to take the measure of his subordinates and inspire them, and, if he is skillful, to learn more about what is going on than simply by reading.

An administrative innovation in the George W. Bush administration was an interagency version of the "directed telescope" that Napoleon and Wellington used in the early nineteenth century. Those commanders would send trusted subordinates to parts of the battlefield to investigate and report back swiftly. In the Bush administration, Lieutenant General Douglas E. Lute, as deputy national security advisor, would go to Iraq and Afghanistan every couple of months for about ten days at a time. I went with him and several other defense and state counterparts, to have meetings in the capitals and then get a sense for what was transpiring in the field. It proved an invaluable means for keeping a key level of government—the level that supported the cabinet sectaries and the president—in close touch with the field.

Special envoys, a feature of the Obama administration, seem to me a less promising innovation. To whom do they really report? The president or the secretary of state? If they come from the State Department, how do they interact with the Department of Defense? What territory do they cover? Which bureaucracy do you put behind them? The deputy national security adviser position specifically for the management of a war has proven a far more effective way of coordinating the government's efforts. The Bush administration, in this respect, returned to the practice of the late Johnson administration in recreating the role played by Robert W. Komer.

In my book, *Supreme Command*, I advocate an unequal dialogue between civilian and military leadership. Unequal because the civilians ultimately call the shots, but a dialogue that requires the utmost in military candor with its superiors. The big decisions in any war—to include COIN— will prove contentious. There was very divided military opinion about the surge in Iraq in 2007, for example. The civilians must seek out those divisions and have them argued out in front of the president. But none of this should take place in public, particularly with regard to irregular warfare disputes about big issues of strategy that have large and disturbing effects on what transpires on the ground. Friends, enemies, and most important those who have not yet made up their minds watch CNN (Cable News Network). In particular they seek to discover how much resolution American leaders have. In all wars, including these, brains matter. But if your enemies, your allies, and your own people begin to think you lack heart, no clever strategies or brilliantly conceived doctrine will yield up victory.

Part II
Brigade and Regimental Command

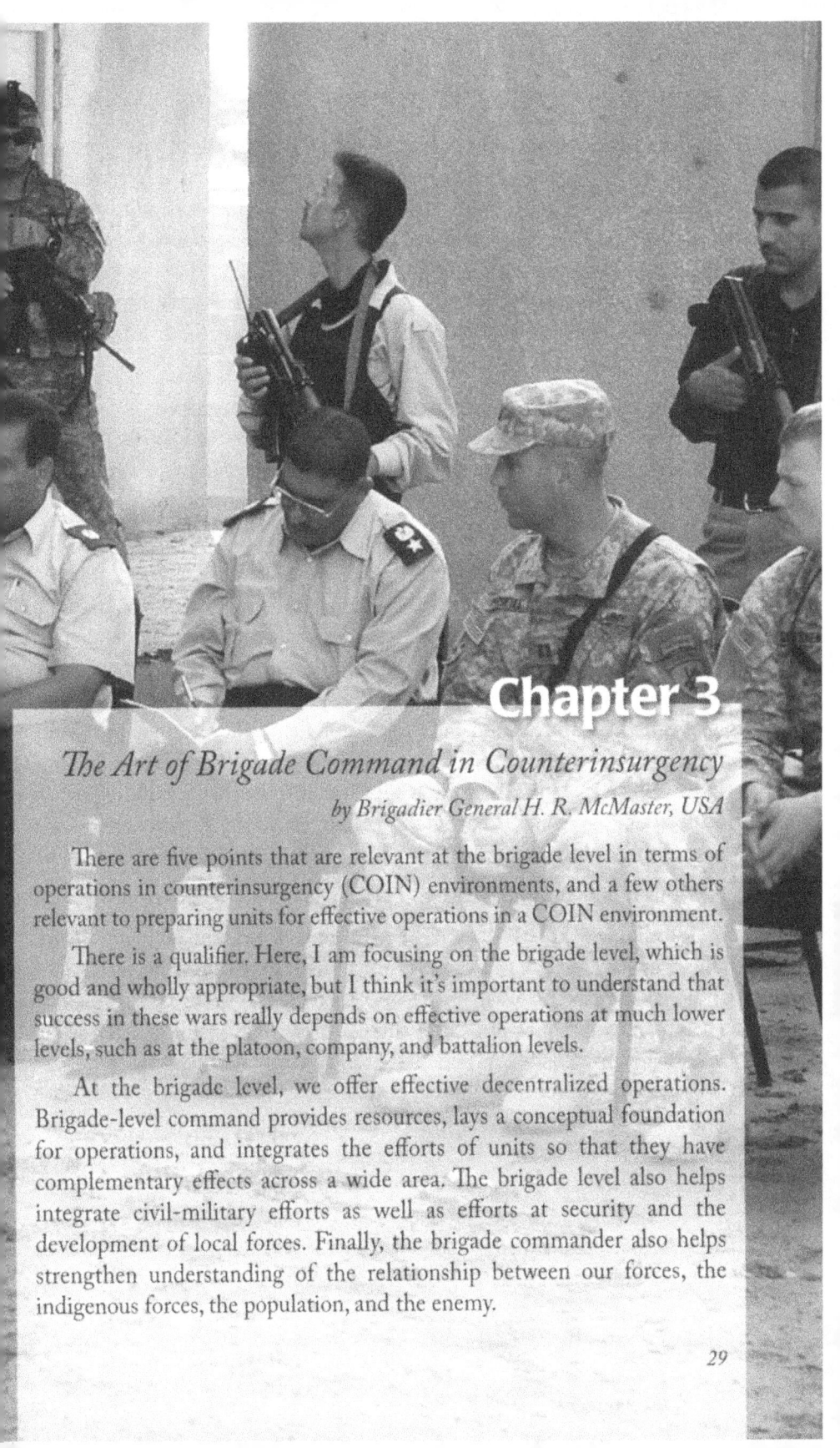

Chapter 3

The Art of Brigade Command in Counterinsurgency

by Brigadier General H. R. McMaster, USA

There are five points that are relevant at the brigade level in terms of operations in counterinsurgency (COIN) environments, and a few others relevant to preparing units for effective operations in a COIN environment.

There is a qualifier. Here, I am focusing on the brigade level, which is good and wholly appropriate, but I think it's important to understand that success in these wars really depends on effective operations at much lower levels, such as at the platoon, company, and battalion levels.

At the brigade level, we offer effective decentralized operations. Brigade-level command provides resources, lays a conceptual foundation for operations, and integrates the efforts of units so that they have complementary effects across a wide area. The brigade level also helps integrate civil-military efforts as well as efforts at security and the development of local forces. Finally, the brigade commander also helps strengthen understanding of the relationship between our forces, the indigenous forces, the population, and the enemy.

I think we are in danger of exaggerating the level of agency that brigade commanders actually have in counterinsurgencies. There is also the danger of underestimating the relative importance of local leaders. For example, Iraqi General Najim Abed Al-Jabouri was the real hero of what we were able to achieve in Tal Afar. He provided the leadership that was necessary to move various communities toward the kind of accommodation necessary to stop the sectarian civil war and allowed us to accomplish what we did alongside the Iraqis.

The first thing I'd like to discuss about effective operations is planning. We have a process in place that was developed in the 1990s. It is an oversystematized checklist that sometimes can be regarded as a substitute for thought—and that's the most dangerous thing that could happen in the COIN environment.

One of the things our Army is doing now is focusing on design, framing problems, and thinking broadly about them. All actions need to be based on a political strategy. Failing to do this means security efforts can run counter to political goals. As David Galula observed, politics becomes an active instrument of operation in a COIN. And so intricate is the interplay between the political and military actions that they cannot be totally separated. Every military move must be weighed with regard to its political effects and vice versa. Brigade leaders need to impart a high degree of understanding across their organization about how their operations contribute to the success of the political outcomes in the area of operation.

This is relevant to the debates between COIN and raiding operations.

A raiding approach to COIN has its roots in strategic bombing theory. This is an easy way out of a complex situation. It has its roots also in the idea of nodal analysis that was popular in the 1990s. This posits that if you look at an enemy organization—and these are conventional organizations—establish what their key nodes are, and attack those nodes, then the organization will collapse. This has been grafted to the problems of terrorism and insurgency that we face today. The raiding approach is problematic because it fails to address the fundamental causes of violence and insecurity. It does not address defeating the enemy because one has to defeat the enemy in relation to securing the population in a COIN. In many ways, the raiding approach actually aids the enemy because the actions can strengthen the enemy's disinformation and propaganda campaign.

The raiding approach is appealing. It allows military officers to get at the enemy and acquire immediate feedback. The commander obtains metrics out of the raids, such as how many leaders the attack killed and captured. But the danger is that a commander can confuse activity with progress. It is only part of the solution, and in extreme cases can actually be detrimental to the commander's efforts.

Thus, the conceptual foundation needs to be joined with the political strategy.

Now I will turn to the five keys to effective operations at the brigade level.

The first is situational understanding. The wars of the 1990s have been a corrective to what you might call the orthodoxy of defense transformation in the revolution in military affairs. We understand now that war is complex. War is complex and uncertain because of all sorts of factors. The ethnic, tribal, sectarian dimensions and dynamics at the local area that we are confronting and how those influence the relative strength of our efforts in combination with the indigenous leaders and forces we are working with relative to those of the enemy stand as key elements of current warfare.

During the 1990s, however, the Army's capstone document on situational understanding stipulated that command-and-control systems would enable leaders to know more than ever before about the activities in their battlespace. They would have accurate information regarding the civil population, weather, terrain, and the locations of both friendlies and the enemy. Consequently, the need for forces in a particular area would be greatly reduced.

What we have learned since is that human, psychological, political, and cultural dimensions keep war firmly in the realm of uncertainty. What we have to do is figuratively and literally fight to achieve situational understanding. Preparation is critical to achieving this. Learning the history of a particular area is immensely important. Situational understanding comes from the bottom up. It comes from interacting with the population and effective reconnaissance operations. Every mission that we conduct in Iraq or Afghanistan is either an area-security or an area-reconnaissance mission to confirm or deny something, so it is important to maintain competencies in reconnaissance and collection of human intelligence.

It is important to see and understand the enemy's network structure. It is important to understand how the enemy network bridges into government, security forces, and illicit and criminal networks so that we can understand the whole problem and how the enemy links the military battleground with the all-important political battleground. These are the battlegrounds that exist in government and security institutions

The other battleground is that of perception, information, and strategic communication. The goals are to understand the nature of the enemy's disinformation and propaganda campaign and understand why that message might resonate with the population. The impact of the enemy's message on the population must be understood before you can effectively counter their campaign.

There is a broad range of questions brigade commanders should always ask themselves. As Sun Tzu postulated, leaders need to understand the enemy strategy to defeat that strategy. To do that, commanders need to understand the enemy's sources of strength and support so they can isolate the enemy from them. These sources are both physical and psychological. Brigade commanders need to understand what the enemy's vulnerabilities and weaknesses are so they can attack those vulnerabilities with both physical force and an effective psychological information campaign.

No matter how effective we are at understanding and learning about an environment, we are not going to know more about Iraq than the Iraqis or more about Afghanistan than the Afghans. Therefore, the most important thing to do in terms of situational understanding is to open a dialogue with the people who live there. In these areas, people are trying to influence you as well as inform you. If a commander understands enough about the dynamics, he can evaluate the sources of information and triangulate issues. I believe that everything we want to know about Iraq and Afghanistan can be discovered by asking the people who are already cooperating with us. The most important approach may be consulting with and listening to indigenous leaders and to the broader population as a whole.

Alongside situational understanding, the second element of effective brigade command is to conduct effective military operations. As noted, these are largely area-security and area-reconnaissance operations. It is important to relentlessly pursue the enemy and to overwhelm him in every engagement. Some have created the false dilemma that in regular wars (that term is vague and imprecise) the goal is to destroy the enemy and in irregular wars the goal is to hand out frozen chickens and Beanie Babies to win over the population. In fact, we are facing brutal, determined, murderous enemies who now can avail themselves of capabilities that were only previously in fielded forces in terms of armor penetrating capability and explosive power. So, there is no substitute for the combat prowess of our forces and our ability to defeat the enemy in every engagement. Nevertheless, it is important to make sure that you inculcate in your unit the judgment and understanding that you have to apply firepower with discipline and discrimination. It is important that commanders maintain focus on combined air-ground arms because what this enemy banks on is being able to make and break contact on their own terms. Brigade commanders want to gain and maintain contact with enemy forces by ensuring that they position units at all times in area security and reconnaissance operations and that they mutually support and talk to each other, and can immediately respond to any situation. The units will ensure that the enemy cannot break contact and has to subsequently respond to multiple forces, approaching from multiple forms of contact: air, ground, overwhelming direct fire, infantry, and mobile protective firepower.

So, all arms doctrine works. Contrary to the general opinion that we are losing some capabilities in our force because of the enemy we are fighting, we still have a high degree of combined arms competency at the company and battalion levels.

The third element of capable brigade command in COIN operations is effective information operations, which entails a wide range of components. Commanders have to expose the enemy's brutality, clarify their intentions, counter the enemy's disinformation campaigns, and bolster the legitimacy of their allied forces. They need to address the fears and aspirations of communities and send a simple, clear message to the population.

The fourth component of command is to achieve unity of effort with indigenous leaders. Effective brigade commanders have to work together with the local security, civil, and political leadership. This involves building and understanding relationships of mutual trust and common purpose. There needs to be an understanding of where interests might diverge and anticipating these differences so the common enemy cannot take advantage of these disagreements.

The fifth element is that brigade leaders need to consolidate their units' gains. In a COIN, we cannot afford to have transitory and temporary successes that are quickly reversed by the enemy. Efforts of consolidation include supporting local governance; establishing the rule of law; rekindling hope among the population; getting basic services running; and, most important, building indigenous police and army forces. These forces need to be able to deal with current and future threats and enjoy the legitimacy and trust of the population.

Chapter 4

Brigade Command in Counterinsurgency Operations: Lessons from the Iraq War

by Colonel Peter R. Mansoor, USA (Retired)

Command in counterinsurgency (COIN) operations exhibits many of the same characteristics as command in high-intensity, conventional warfare, but there are many added considerations that make the job more complex, if not more difficult. Success in both types of operations requires inspired leadership. Commanders must balance mission accomplishment with soldier welfare. They must synchronize the contributions of supporting arms and services to maximize the effectiveness of the force. The enemy, while using different tactics, still gets a vote. Despite these similarities, the job of a commander in COIN operations is made more complex by the numerous, varied skills required to achieve success. It is not true, as Army Chief of Staff General George H. Decker stated to President John F. Kennedy, that "any good soldier can handle guerrillas"; this is not the case with guerrillas who are competent and backed by a popular insurgency.[1] Indeed, commanders in COIN operations have to focus on more than just killing the enemy and taking and holding ground, as in conventional warfighting. Commanders battling an insurgency must complement security operations by developing and engaging local political leaders, improving the economy to put people to work and eliminating joblessness as an excuse for supporting the insurgents, developing local governments to provide the population with essential services, and conducting an informational campaign that is critical to success and not just an adjunct of combat operations. Commanders must orchestrate the varied and essential efforts of interagency, international, and nongovernmental organizations. Furthermore, they must do this while decentralizing authority and empowering junior leaders upon whose shoulders victory or defeat at the all-important local level rests. After examining the many and varied tasks that fall the way of a commander in COIN operations, one must agree with T. E. Lawrence's statement: "Irregular warfare is far more intellectual than a bayonet charge."[2]

Building Relationships

Perhaps the most important facet of command in COIN operations is the development of relationships with local leaders and other influential people. Unless supported by a strong outside power, insurgents ultimately must gain and maintain the support of the people to overturn the existing government. The engagement of local elites is therefore critical to influencing the population to support one side or the other in this struggle for legitimacy, especially in highly tribal societies where people tend to adhere more closely to familial and social groupings. These elites may include politicians, military and police leaders, religious leaders, or informal leaders from the business or educational communities or other groupings. The real leader of a community may not initially be readily apparent, so the commander must work to understand the power relationships at work and seek to engage the real leaders of the people. Indeed, T. E. Lawrence's admonition to his fellow officers applies to U.S. officers in Iraq and

---

[1] Andrew F. Krepinevich Jr., *The Army and Vietnam* (Baltimore: Johns Hopkins University Press, 1986), 37.

[2] T. E. Lawrence, "The Evolution of a Revolt," *Army Quarterly and Defence Journal*, I:1 (October 1920).

Afghanistan today as well: "Go easy just for the first few weeks. A bad start is difficult to atone for, and the Arabs form their judgments on externals that we ignore. When you have reached the inner circle in a tribe, you can do as you please with yourself and them."[3]

Engaging the local community is a team effort in more ways than one. Unless a commander has excellent linguistic abilities, he/she must find a talented interpreter and learn how to use him/her properly. Handled correctly, a good interpreter can be an extremely valuable asset to a commander and can assist in evaluating body language and context as well as the spoken word. In crucial situations the commander should not be afraid to have the interpreter clarify a conversation, for mistranslations can prove deadly in more ways than one.[4]

The task of establishing and nurturing relationships with local elites cannot be delegated to the civil affairs officer or another person. The local people know who is in charge in a given area and will seek to engage that leader in a close relationship. A commander has *wasta*, the Arabic word for influence, and local elites will seek to capitalize on their relationship with the commander to share in this power. In many societies, personal relationships lead to political support, business dealings, and other important associations that can influence the outcome of a COIN conflict. The commander must spend a significant amount of time fostering these relationships and not view such time as detracting from seemingly more important duties.

After a tour in Iraq from June 2003 to July 2004 as the commander of the Army's 1st Brigade, 1st Armored Division, I returned with my unit to Germany to reconstitute and retrain the organization in preparation for its next deployment to the Land of the Two Rivers. After a year of repairing and replacing equipment, integrating new replacements, and retraining, the brigade conducted a rotation in June 2004 at the Combat Maneuver Training Center in Hohenfels, Germany. This ten-day exercise combined COIN training with a few days of conventional combat against opposing forces configured as a hybrid insurgent/conventional force. Local German civilians played the role of villagers, local leaders, and other people with

---

[3] T. E. Lawrence, "Twenty-Seven Articles," *Arab Bulletin*, 20 August 1917.
[4] For an example, see Peter R. Mansoor, *Baghdad at Sunrise: A Brigade Commander's War in Iraq* (New Haven: Yale University Press, 2008), 214–16 and 227–28.

whom a force would have to engage in COIN operations. As I did in Iraq during my previous tour, I spent a considerable amount of time engaging the local "leaders" in this training scenario. During one eventful meeting, local "elites" pressed me for favors and showered me with complaints, to which I calmly responded. After five hours, I was just getting warmed up (many engagements in Iraq had lasted well into the evening hours); the locals grew tired, said their goodbyes, and departed. The observers commented later that the meeting had gone three times longer than any previous engagement, which had always ended with the brigade commander excusing himself to attend to "more important duties." I was used to delegating those other functions to subordinate leaders; to me, the engagement of these local elites was my most important task.

Communicating with the Public

In COIN warfare, perceptions are often more important than reality. If the local people believe the insurgents are winning, then they are winning. If the American people believe we are losing, then we are losing, despite the realities of the battlefield. The Tet Offensive in 1968 is a case in point. The offensive was a huge tactical and operational success for U.S. and South Vietnamese forces, which succeeded in eliminating a large chunk of the Viet Cong in less than six months. Tet was a strategic failure, however, because the American people believed the offensive showed the enemy had far greater strength than they had been told, and therefore the pressure to withdraw U.S. forces from the conflict became unstoppable.

Because of the importance of these perceptions, a commander in COIN operations must build an information campaign to influence the local population and a public affairs campaign to inform the wider audience before embarking on operations. The most important piece of the information campaign is to build a narrative—a key means through which the counterinsurgents can express their purpose to the people. To be effective, the narrative must be short and easily understood. In Iraq, for instance, al-Qaeda operatives used a form of the following narrative to appeal to Sunni tribesmen: "You're Sunni, we're Sunni, we both hate the Persians [i.e., Shiites] and the Americans—let's fight them together." Stories linked to Islamic history or the 1920 Iraqi tribal rebellion against the British also played heavily in insurgent narratives. The American narrative in

2003—that we came to Iraq as liberators to free the oppressed Iraqi people—was not believed by many Iraqis who suspected more nefarious motives, be they realpolitik or the seizure of Iraqi oil. A narrative that worked was, "Let's rebuild Iraq together." When an Iraqi would ask me where I was from, my answer was Rusafa, the Baghdad province that housed my brigade headquarters. Unfortunately, the withdrawal of U.S. forces from their forward operating bases inside Baghdad in spring 2004 invalidated this narrative because Iraqis inside Baghdad viewed the withdrawal suspiciously, rather than accepting the stated motive that we were merely empowering local Iraqi security forces that in reality did not exist.

Once a commander has built a narrative (and tested it out on the local people), he/she must use every means available to communicate it to the population: TV, radio, newspapers, flyers, and even the rumor mill. The key is to use the means most widely available to the people. In Iraq, this meant using satellite TV to broadcast messages, something that U.S. forces were quite unprepared to do early in the war.

A commander must engage the media and encourage his/her subordinates to do likewise. The public affairs plan must cover all media—local, national (e.g., Al Iraqiya), regional (e.g., Al Jazeera), international (e.g., BBC [British Broadcasting Corporation]), and U.S. (e.g., Fox News and CNN [Cable News Network]). The media will report on events regardless of whether or not a commander engages reporters, so it is best to suit up and get in the game. If you don't play, you lose by default. The best policy is to be forthright; don't spin news or put lipstick on pigs. A commander should demand three things of the media: factual accuracy, the correct context for stories, and proper characterization of the situation and people involved. When the media falls short of its professional standards, the commander should engage and demand clarifications and retractions as appropriate. This is a two-way street; the commander should also be forthright with his/her statements and issue follow-ups as necessary to ensure the media is informed of a developing situation.

Combat Operations

Commanders of conventional forces, trained in high-intensity combat operations and taught to be aggressive in seeking out and destroying the enemy, must reorient their thinking for COIN warfare. The mission in this type of conflict is often focused on protection of the population, with killing the enemy serving as a byproduct of the primary objective. Too much force used too aggressively can alienate the population when collateral damage kills or wounds innocent civilians and damages property. Even with the best-trained forces, some collateral damage will occur. Commanders must ensure innocent victims are quickly and appropriately compensated for their loss. Proportionality in the use of force is critical; commanders must set the tone to ensure the ethical conduct of their troops. Given the sudden and horrific nature of some attacks, leaders must curb the baser instinct of soldiers to blame bystanders for the deaths and grievous injuries of their comrades.

The commander should look at every situation from the enemy's point of view and engage his/her intelligence officer in a constant and ongoing dialogue concerning the enemy's capabilities and intentions. As is the case with conventional combat operations, the enemy in COIN warfare has a say in what happens. Commanders must consciously curb their more aggressive instincts. Acting too quickly on intelligence, for instance, can prove counterproductive. Target development in COIN warfare takes more time, since human intelligence is often the basis for decision making and it is, more often than not, slow to develop. Commanders should sequence operations in time and space, a method I call *cadenced targeting*. This basically means commanders should slow the targeting cycle down to allow intelligence to develop and reduce the number of false leads, which can result in the detention of innocent people. In this regard, commanders should personally examine their system for detention and interrogation to ensure it is not only effective, but also humane. Commanders should be personally involved in reviewing interrogation results and judging which detainees should be sent outside the brigade area for incarceration and not just take the word of the staff judge advocate or intelligence officer, as good as these officers might be.

Brigade commanders should focus on the larger picture and work to support battalion and company commanders with additional assets. The key is to decentralize operations and not do the battalion and company commanders' jobs for them. Micromanagement of COIN operations will invariably lead to failure, as a single commander cannot make the myriad decisions needed on a daily basis by junior leaders in the field and on the streets. The brigade commander should, however, ensure consistency in policies and procedures throughout the area of operations. The local people will notice differences in various unit areas, and insurgents will take advantage of any gaps and seams they find.

Most important, the brigade commander must ensure that other security forces in his/her area are integrated into operations. A commander should establish good working relationships with any Special Operations Forces in the area, even if they do not fall under his/her span of command and control. The commander should pay close attention to the development of and coordination with local security forces, even to the extent of using brigade assets to support the advisory effort in the area. In the end, as T. E. Lawrence notes, it is more important that indigenous forces execute tolerably than it is for U.S. forces to execute perfectly, "for it is their war and you are to help them, not to win it for them."[5]

Humanitarian and Civic Action

COIN warfare may be more about winning the confidence and trust of the people than it is about winning their hearts and minds. Security is certainly a large part of that equation, for the fundamental basis for the legitimacy of any governing authority is the ability to secure the people. Beyond security, however, people everywhere want an adequate standard of living (as defined by the local culture), a means to provide for their family's welfare, and a decent place to live. Counterinsurgents can increase the legitimacy of the local governing authority by assisting it in providing the people with a decent quality of life.

Commanders work to gain the trust and confidence of the population through humanitarian and civic action programs. The commander should not delegate these activities to his/her civil affairs officer, for they are far too important. One recent innovation that has proven successful in coordinating these activities is the Embedded Provincial Reconstruction Team (EPRT), a means for linking interagency assets with military forces on the local level. The commander and the EPRT leader should work closely together. One technique is for the brigade commander and EPRT leader to co-chair regular meetings on humanitarian and civic actions that are separate from the targeting meetings held to discuss kinetic operations. Separate meetings

---

[5] Lawrence, "Twenty-Seven Articles."

will provide humanitarian and civic actions with adequate time and attention, while the commander's presence will ensure that the outcomes mesh with other activities in the brigade area, including combat operations.

As General David H. Petraeus noted, in COIN warfare, money is ammunition.[6] But the corollary is that money is an unguided projectile that a commander must aim at the right target. The temptation is to tackle a number of projects that will make life in the community better, under the assumption that the people will give the counterinsurgent forces credit for the improvement in their quality of life. Such is not the case. In some instances insurgents or militias will take credit for projects accomplished with U.S. dollars, as was the case in Sadr City for much of the Iraq War, where Muqtada al-Sadr's *Jaish al-Mahdi* militia claimed it was responsible for projects accomplished with money allocated from the U.S. Commander's Emergency Response Program. In areas under insurgent intimidation or control, the local people may accept reconstruction activities, but the resulting thankfulness will not change their behavior one iota. In COIN warfare, gratitude theory (i.e., "you do things for me and I'll do things for you") does not work, as insurgent threats trump counterinsurgent good deeds. Instead, commanders must use money and reconstruction activities to consciously force the people to choose which side to support, perhaps by making the local community provide a portion of the funds for specific projects. People with some "skin in the game" will do more to ensure their equity is protected. Commanders should also include local leaders in the decision-making process for civic action projects. Getting buy-in and ownership of these activities is an important step that commanders cannot overlook merely because it takes more time to engage local leaders in the process.

Troop Welfare

Troop welfare in COIN operations is not too far removed from troop welfare in high-intensity combat operations, but there are some differences given the fact that a COIN conflict can go on for years. Repeated deployments can wear troops down unless they are provided a decent standard of support. In Iraq I focused on the "5 Ms" of soldier care:

---

[6] LtGen David H. Petraeus, USA, "Learning Counterinsurgency: Observations from Soldiering in Iraq," *Military Review*, January–February 2006.

• Meals: hot chow, varied menus

• Medical: cleanliness and adequacy of medical facilities

• Mail: to include email and phones

• Money: to ensure the home front remained happy

• Morale: latrines, showers, and entertainment

Twelve-month rotations, sometimes extended to as many as fifteen months, can wear down even the hardiest of soldiers, particularly over multiple deployments, so some degree of comfort makes sense.

On the other hand, commanders must also ensure the troops retain an expeditionary mindset in case they need to pack up and move on a moment's notice. During the deployment of the 1st Brigade, 1st Armored Division, to Iraq in 2003–04, there were two operations that required substantial elements of the brigade to deploy within country on short notice: Operation Longstreet in August–September 2003 and Operation Iron Saber in south-central Iraq from April–June 2004. The troops were not so far removed from the initial invasion that they viewed these movements as extraordinary. During the beginning of the surge in February 2007, on the other hand, some soldiers who had grown so accustomed to life on large bases found it initially difficult to adapt to the more austere conditions of joint security stations and combat outposts, with their more primitive quality of life. The soldiers adjusted, but commanders would do well to ensure their troops never lose their expeditionary mindset in the first place.

Indigenous Leadership

Developing competent and supportive indigenous leaders is crucial to COIN warfare, for U.S. forces cannot remain in foreign countries fighting their wars indefinitely. Commanders should work to build trust with local leaders by establishing social and professional connections and treating them as equals (or superiors, if such is the case). Commanders should include local leaders in orders and rehearsals to validate their status as part of the team. Brigade commanders must work to build the competency of local forces in their areas, for their success is of paramount importance. Indigenous leaders have a number of home field advantages, and can capitalize on local intelligence sources; cultural expertise; social connections; and language capabilities, which U.S. commanders would do well to leverage.

There might be situations (such as those that exist today in Afghanistan) where sufficient numbers of competent local leaders simply do not exist to staff the large number of formations needed to prosecute COIN warfare. In this case, the United States might consider staffing local units with U.S. commanders. An Afghan battalion commanded by a U.S. Army or Marine Corps major with a small cadre of officers and noncommissioned officers to fill subordinate command positions would make the creation of effective combat units much easier. U.S. leaders could be changed out over time as competent Afghan leaders emerge from the ranks.

At the same time, a number of local leaders will prove to be unsuitable due to extremism or incompetence. Commanders must weed out extremist/sectarian leaders who would use their forces for nefarious ends (e.g., criminality, sectarian cleansing, death squad activity.). Ideally, the United States would retain hiring and firing authority over the local forces that it helped create, a model advocated by historian and COIN expert Bing West.[7] Realistically, few states will ever cede this piece of sovereignty to the United States, so in practice U.S. leaders must intensively engage local political and military authorities to force them to get rid of the worst of the extremist and incompetent leaders. In September 2007 a report by retired Marine General James L. Jones recommended the dissolution of the Iraqi National Police force due to its highly sectarian behavior. Instead, General Petraeus, commander of Multi National Force–Iraq, worked with Iraqi leaders to clean up the force by changing out every brigade commander and roughly two-thirds of the battalion commanders, some of them twice.[8] By the end of the surge, the Iraqi National Police force, while not a paragon of virtue and still exhibiting sectarian behavior in some areas, was more of an asset than a liability to sustainable stability in Iraq.

---

[7] Francis J. "Bing" West, *The Strongest Tribe: War, Politics, and the Endgame in Iraq* (New York: Random House, 2008), 39–40.

[8] Linda Robinson, *Tell Me How This Ends: General David Petraeus and the Search for a Way Out of Iraq* (New York: PublicAffairs, 2008), 299 and 336.

Overhauling Professional Military Education

The above discussion highlights the incredibly complex nature of command in COIN warfare. Quite frankly, the military did not do terribly well in preparing its leaders for this kind of combat in the run-up to the wars in Afghanistan and Iraq. U.S. military forces have done much to adapt to COIN warfare since then, but need to do more to enhance professional military education (PME) to prepare leaders for these types of conflicts. If PME is so important to the ability of U.S. officers to command forces in COIN warfare—and I think it is—then the U.S. military should once again treat it as a serious career gate, as indeed it was during the interwar period between the end of the Great War (World War I) and the beginning of World War II.

Many of the educational competencies—history, culture, languages—needed in COIN operations are not adequately taught in PME programs. Adding these fields of study to existing PME institutions will merely result in watered-down programs that lack focus. A different solution would be to send more officers to civilian graduate programs in history, cultural anthropology, social sciences, area studies, and similar fields. One suggestion is to take every captain who is selected for early promotion to major and send him/her to a civilian graduate program for twelve to twenty-four months to obtain a master's degree before heading to a command and general staff college for the intermediate-level education. The result of this initiative would be to ensure that nearly every brigade and division commander of the future receives a master's degree from a civilian university along with standard PME, a change that would enhance the intellectual capabilities of U.S. military senior leadership in years to come.

As for PME itself, it is time to ramp up the difficulty level of our command, general staff, and war colleges. Rather than making entrance an inalienable right, we should require officers to pass a rigorous entrance examination. Colleges should break up staff groups where a few officers carry the load and force officers to conduct serious study on their own as well as in small groups. The common scenario used by some institutions that pigeonholes the curriculum into a single area of the world should be eliminated. Further changes should include assigning grades, creating an order of merit list, and rewarding the top 25 percent of the class with the best assignments upon graduation, much as the military academies currently do with their class rankings.

There will be those who complain that such changes are just too hard to implement in a force that is as busy as the military is today. Yet, providing select officers a year to attend a civilian college is no different than granting selected officers a second year after completion of intermediate-level education to attend the School for Advanced Military Studies. To create less pressure to move officers back into line units, Congress should authorize an expanded pool of field grade officers in the force and extend the mandatory retirement age by five years. Furthermore, the Army should eliminate S3/XO (executive officer) assignments as career gates, which creates the time pressure for majors to return to the force where "the real soldiering takes place"—an attitude not shared in other eras in U.S. military history.

Indeed, we could look to the Army's history for an alternative career path. During the 1920s and 1930s, the prize assignment for Army officers was selection for schooling at Fort Leavenworth, Kansas. The course itself was an extremely difficult, five-and-a-half days a week affair. The best officers in each class were then offered follow-on assignments as instructors. The chosen few beyond that were assigned to the Army War College a bit later in their careers. PME in the interwar period was serious business, the critical path to career advancement. When the Army expanded dramatically during World War II, it managed to find enough competent leaders to command its formations, despite the lack of S3/XO time and field experience. More important, its highly educated officer corps provided the backbone for higher level staffs that in most cases performed well in the crucible of war, and that got most of the key strategic decisions during the war right.

The U.S. military would do well to reemphasize PME in the years ahead, for irregular warfare is here to stay, and it is, as T. E. Lawrence claimed, far more intellectual than a bayonet charge.

Chapter 5

Regimental Command in Counterinsurgency

by Brigadier General W. Blake Crowe, USMC

I would like to discuss regimental combat team (RCT) operations. The RCT is a task-organized aggregation. I had the opportunity in June to sit in on a teleconference with Brigadier General Lawrence D. Nicholson, commander of the 2d Marine Expeditionary Brigade in Afghanistan. One of the points he made as he addressed the General Officer Warfighting Program in Quantico, Virginia, is that what he experienced in Iraq and is prepared to experience in Afghanistan is what RCT-2, RCT-7, and my command experienced in 2006–07. These were completely different operations than some regimental commanders in Fallujah faced.

One significant lesson is that counterinsurgency (COIN) environments are not all the same. A village, be it on the western Euphrates River valley, is different from areas right outside of Fallujah. These areas are both about the size of South Carolina, so the operations are distributed over a wide geographic range. The area commanders had relative autonomy, as I did from the Marine Expeditionary Force (MEF) commander. The commanders visited, but I was left to run that area of operations the way I wanted to, working with our two partner Iraqi brigades.

Our area of operations began along the Syrian border and extended down to the Jordanian border. We were also responsible for the MEF security area, which extended to Saudi Arabia. This was a large area and it was not possible to be everywhere. This situation forced us to work with the locals and to work and play well with other units operating in the region, such as the Special Operations Forces (SOF). But there in 2006, we were the surrogate government. We did not have mayors at the time. The provincial governor was in Ramadi and he stayed there. Twice we were able to get him out to western al-Anbar in the year I was there, and it took a regimental-size operation to get him out to cities such as Baghdadi, Haditha, and al-Qa'im. We spent nearly thirty days worth of planning to get him out there because for us he was more important than the president of the United States. I think Marines here would understand that.

Our first mayor came in six months into my deployment in al-Qa'im. Lieutenant Colonel Dale Alford, commander of the 3d Battalion, 6th Marines, was involved in setting the conditions for that success. We didn't have a mayor in Haditha because we had to arrest him. He was an insurgent. We didn't have a mayor in Hit because the previous ones had been killed. So until December 2006, we were the surrogate local government. We learned very quickly that if we allowed the Iraqis to fail to build and provision their security forces, then we would have failed as well. So, we had to step in and fill that surrogate role.

There is a debate concerning these operations and whether or not they are counterinsurgencies, hybrid operations, or distributed operations. We did them all. In al-Qa'im, we conducted what I would call a pure COIN because the conditions had been set by the previous regiment. We were still having major manned gun, tank rounds, and combined arms in downtown Hit with more than one hundred surging on twelve- to fifteen-man positions. And so we did the whole gamut out there. Phasing, synchronizing, supporting, and enabling formed what I thought was my primary role there.

Every battalion commander wants to be the main effort. Every regimental or brigade commander wants to be the main effort. We weren't the main effort in Iraq. And every battalion could not be the main effort, and that's the hard thing for people to reconcile. How come I'm not getting all these assets?

When I was in Afghanistan, I received everything. We were one Marine battalion attached to the Army and we were given everything. In Iraq, I had five battalions in my command and one reduced Force Reconnaissance company commanded by six lieutenant colonels. At least one unit is not going to get what they want in a timely fashion. The battalions, companies, and platoons had autonomy, but autonomy doesn't mean that they operated independently. That's where synchronizing comes in. It means going out and working very close to the battalions and blurring the borders between zones of responsibility and forcing commanders to get together and have a cup of coffee. Just as we needed to have tea with the local nationals, we also needed to do that among ourselves. We did that very well with the SOF. I put liaisons with the national-level SOF. I put liaisons with the white SOF. Every morning at 0800, I had the advanced operating base commander from the SOF detachment in my office with the signal and human intelligence. It was basically our own little fusion cell. We established an ad-hoc tactical fusion center at the regimental level, and so I would advocate that for future RCT operations.

As in all American military campaigns, a lot of manpower gets sucked up into the higher headquarters. These tend to have more people than the battalions on the ground. The Marine Corps has evolved to a point that intelligence cells are down to company level. People are being pulled at the higher headquarters, whereas we're feeding the beast. I think the beast shouldn't be higher. I think the beast should be at the level of the lance corporal, corporal, sergeant leading the patrol, and the lieutenant out on point.

I mentioned quickly the key traits of people. We put a lot of emphasis on that during the entire deployment. We didn't wait for policy to come down. A former boss of mine said, "Common sense is not a common virtue." I think you figure out what you need to do out there and you do it. And you work with the commanding general staff to figure out the legal ways of doing it.

As an example, we raised close to 4,000 police officers. I waited a year and was told the police stations are coming. They never did. So we created expeditionary forward operating bases, because that way I could use Marine Corps money. I could put police in them, although they could not be designated official Iraqi Police stations. If it was designated as such, you would get reported because it would not be official. So, there are things that you have to do. It's not selective disobedience of orders, but rather a creative way of getting the mission accomplished.

We had two force protection measures: the American standard and what was acceptable to the Iraqis. That was unacceptable to me as a commander. The first time you go to a scene where you've lost a soldier, it does not matter what uniform he's wearing. He is one of ours. He was bought in to serve with us and I don't care what nationality he is. We needed to build it to one standard: checkpoints, force protection, food, weapons, ammunition, all the way down. They fight with us and we're going to treat them to our standard. That's just nonnegotiable.

I was at Training and Education Command prior to taking over the regiment. The feedback loop is pretty fast in the Marine Corps. It's kind of like this. General James N. Mattis picking up the phone and calling Major General T. S. Jones and saying, "Build us something—Matilda Village is closed at March Air Force Base—build us something at Twentynine Palms for General Stephen T. Johnson and II MEF to have when they go back over. Do it now." And we did it.

The feedback loop to the training and education continuum, through the School of Infantry and Expeditionary Warfare School, are producing the finest officers we've ever had. Can we be better? Yes, we can. And how we can do that? I was very fortunate as regimental commander to have the assessments of every battalion and their company commanders at the Mojave Viper predeployment operation training exercises. When I arrived in Iraq, I hadn't trained with them because we deploy a little differently than the Army. I didn't know these individuals. However, the assessments were almost 99 percent spot on to what kind of unit I was receiving. Was it a learning organization? Were they not a learning organization? And it went down by personalities.

The only thing I would suggest for improving that system is that we do a proper, credible evaluation at home station prior to getting to Mojave Viper, to act on some of the recommendations that are made here, picking the right company and battalion commanders who are identified early in the process. We can't identify it at Mojave Viper because in many cases the battalions deploy within thirty days after predeployment exercises.

My recommendation is that we need to figure out the methodology.

Part III
Battalion Command

Chapter 6

The Art of Battalion Command in Counterinsurgency: A Discussion

Honorable Francis J. "Bing" West; Colonel David J. Furness, USMC;
Colonel William M. Jurney, USMC; and Colonel Julian Dale Alford, USMC

Francis J. "Bing" West

This panel deals with fighting in the trenches, the tackling and blocking that happens up front in the line. What you have received about these gentlemen really does not tell you the reason that they're here. When we were in Ramadi, a lot of people, including myself, didn't think it could be brought under control. William M. Jurney was the battalion commander who did it. And Dale Alford, of course, is a legend because he went out to al-Qa'im, 250 miles from Baghdad, the Syrian border town that was just totally out of control. With one battalion, he established not only control, but managed to work with the tribes so that after he left, it remained quiet. Everyone felt that on the Syrian border this just couldn't be done. And so you do have the opportunity this morning of listening to a few people whose credentials are just absolutely remarkable.

I've been to Afghanistan four times. I was there in April and May 2009 and again in June and July 2009 and went on about forty combat patrols up north and down south. What really concerns me—and it's very, very simple—every valley has a mountain. And all the mountains are controlled by the Taliban, and the watchers are everywhere. No American or Afghan patrol leaves the wire without being watched and reported on the whole way. And I'll tell you H. R. [McMaster], that really concerns me because it indicates that there's a substrata of that society that we're dealing with, and if everywhere you go they're watching you all the time, this is a big, big problem.

The way in which all the firefights had been taking place up until the last couple of months was very simple. We were fighting Apaches who remained very well hidden. You'd never get a distinct target and generally the ranges were 400 to 600 meters. This is in the Korengal, and we're firing at targets that were firing at us 600 meters away, but you had to go down a valley and up the other side, so there's no way you could close with them. So, we automatically called in air strikes.

General H. R. McMaster was talking about company commanders having these indirect fires at their disposal. Yes, every single patrol has it, but we now have a new tactical directive that says, "Knock off using most of it because you're also killing civilians." That leads to a very big problem about what takes its place. And there is another element in Afghanistan that concerns me. In Ganjgal, we looked back from our MRAP [mine resistant, ambush protected vehicle] to see kids coming out right behind us putting down rocks in order to trap us. We did everything according to the book on counterinsurgency, and they betrayed the Marines and Afghan soldiers when they went into that village and that's why they were all killed.

So there are some hearts and minds that you're just not going to win. The politics of each valley differ, but every single battlespace owner, every single battalion commander that we now have in Afghanistan, could come to this meeting, give you a map of his area, and take a red line and show you the areas where he cannot go without getting into a firefight.

The dilemma that we're going to be facing in the future is that the more we have constrained our indirect fires, which has been the principal way in which we were doing this, you leave two big questions dangling out there at the battalion level: how do you finish the firefights, and where are we going?

Right now we're not finishing firefights, so we're basically not doing damage to the enemy. The enemy isn't doing damage to us because we have our armor. But we now have attrition warfare. We don't have mobility warfare. The Taliban run circles around us because they're not wearing heavy armor. They're in much better shape, they're in incredible shape. And as a result, they hold the initiative. They decide when to initiate a firefight. They decide when to stop the firefight. And we react to them, and we're not finishing the firefights. So we're not killing the enemy.

Now, are we arresting the enemy? Excuse me, I used to say "detain" or something. Now we say "arrest." No. The Afghans arrest practically no one. And the average number of arrests for an American battalion is one person every two months.

So we're not killing them and we're not arresting them. Thus, the blocking and tackling that are fundamentally essential are right now lacking. We can put in more troops, but my concern about this is, if we don't find a way of finishing these fights, we could be having this conversation a year to two years from now and the Taliban would still be intact.

That leads to the second question: where are we going? Basically, if we're managing what we measure, we have some adjusting to do in what it is we think we're going to be doing in Afghanistan. The question is, "What is our theory of victory?" It seems to me if you read the assessment that General H. R. McMaster and others worked on, you read the assessment that General Stanley A. McChrystal came out with the other day and you read it very carefully, its theory of victory is not victory—it's transition. And when you look for how we transition, it becomes a little bit fuzzy. If transition is the name of the game, then the very best paper I've ever seen on it was written by Major General Robert B. Neller when he was an obscure brigadier general out in Okinawa. It's the best single paper that I've ever seen about how you transition. But the problem we now have with the Afghan Army is very simple. We built it in our image. They're all wearing armor. They're all wearing helmets. They are no more mobile than we are. When you get into the firefight, they immediately turn to the advisor because only the advisor is permitted to call in the indirect fires. The minute you call in the indirect fires, you're positioning the troops, you become the leader in the combat.

The Afghan leaders are absolutely the key to the success, but Mark Moyar has this fascinating section in his book where he interviewed something like 250 advisors. They estimated that 65 percent of all Afghan battalions have poor leaders. And yet, our advisors have about zero effect on promotions in the Afghan system. I know that Peter Mansoor said Bing West is for these joint promotion boards, but General David H. Petraeus had another way of doing it. I think we're out of time for being gentle in Afghanistan, and if we're going to make a difference, I think we have to get more control over who's in charge in the Afghan Army.

Colonel David J. Furness

Battalion command in counterinsurgency operations has kind of a broad left and right lateral limit, so I'll confine my comments to actions that we took prior to and while in combat.

There are no new ideas here. There's nothing earth shattering. Most were borrowed from peers who I respect, like the two gentlemen to my right. These are things I learned while I served on the staff of the 1st Marine Division in 2003 and 2004, and things that I read through self-study. I tried to apply them in a dynamic environment, and here are some of the lessons that I learned.

My experience is all based in southern Baghdad in 2005 when I was commanding officer of Battalion Landing Team 1st Battalion, 1st Marines, the ground combat element of the 15th Marine Expeditionary Unit. And then in 2006 at a place north of Fallujah, Karmah, or "Bad Karmah," as we liked to refer to it. But it was all eastern al-Anbar province, western Baghdad.

Karmah is about 10 kilometers northeast of Fallujah. It is surrounded by small villages that were my principal population centers in and around the area. I had part of the northern Zadon, which was kind of a no-man's-land at times. But this is the area in 2006 that I operated in when I was attached to Regimental Combat Team 5.

It is a decentralized fight. Everybody agrees with that. And if you're going to be successful in a decentralized fight, you have to operate on commander's intent. No one will dispute that. But how do you get people to understand intent and be able to use intent? No one really tells you about that.

I learned from watching General James N. Mattis at the division level go down to the PFC [private first class] level and just embed his ideas, his thought process, what was important to him, down to the private. I said okay, that's what I have to do when I get a battalion command.

Everybody has a philosophy of command, philosophy of training, philosophies of this and that, and I'm no different. I came into command with them and spent a lot of time trying to craft a language that actually meant something. I handed those things out. I had a one-pager for the Marines and NCOs [noncommissioned officers]. I had a more complex, little longer version for staff NCOs and officers. I gave them out. I had them read them, and then in groups of twenty, platoon size, I went around after they were read and we had discussions. We had team meetings. What am I talking about when I say this? What does this mean? What am I telling you to do?

You try to operationalize intent because you want them to understand it so that when they're at that point where they have to make a decision and no one's around and it's only corporal so and so, he can do it. He knows what Furness would want him to do and that's probably the only thing—if that's the only thing—he can remember, it's something he can fall back on and, hopefully, it gets him through that difficult decision.

So, I think that's the most important thing that you have to do right up front as a battalion commander. You've got to put your fingerprints on your unit right from the start, the first day you grab the guidon. And once they understand it, then you reinforce that every day by what General Charles C. Krulak used to call "leadership by walking around." You've got to get out of your office, you've got to get away from the computer, and you've got to talk to your Marines, and sailors—where they work, what they care about, and everything they do. You give them a little "that's the way I want it done," pat on the back, or "hey, next time you do it, how about his way, you're doing a great job." But you have to imprint what you feel is important into their brain housing groups.

The next point, individual small unit discipline, is the key in counterinsurgency. General Anthony Zinni once said that elite units are better at counterinsurgency because they have greater discipline. And discipline is what's going to give you restraint, which is going to give you discrimination in the use of fires, and it's the bedrock on which everything else is built. So you have to instill it. With our op tempo going one hundred miles an hour, discipline can sometimes fall by the wayside because we don't have time to correct it right on the spot. You know, "We'll get to that later." Well, you can't do that.

Somebody said, "If you could do anything to a battalion to prepare it for counterinsurgency operations, what would you do?" I thought for a minute and said, "I'd put them through recruit training, all as a group, and let a bunch of gunnies with Smokey Bear hats just beat discipline into them for 13 weeks." The tactics are fairly simple but the discipline is hard to instill.

I had a long talk with staff NCOs and NCOs about their role in helping me attain a level of individual and small-unit discipline that would carry the day when we got into this dispersed dynamic environment. And I also told them, "Your discipline will be your hallmark and it's the only information operations message that as a small unit in Iraq you control. You control how you're perceived by the population, the way you walk out the gate, the way you wear your gear, how you carry your weapons, they instantly perceive that and that's the only information operations message that you control as a small battalion in this big, wide, long war."

The thing I focused most on in predeployment preparations is NCO training because, again, I think General McMaster said it: "That's where it's going to be won—corporals, sergeants, lieutenants." That's where you have to focus because that's who is going to be way out there on the edge of the empire, the pointy end of the spear, like we say. Those are the Marines who are going to make those tough calls, and if they're not trained to deal with that type of decision making, if they don't have the requisite excellence in their weapons handling and their small unit tactics, they're not going to be able to do that job.

So, we ran a battalion in-house through the predeployment training program. We called it the Leaders' Course because there were some lance corporals who were filling NCO billets that received the training as well. The bottom line was we wanted to control how Marines would be led in 1st Battalion, 1st Marines. We didn't have enough quotas for the great sergeants' course or the division squad leaders' course. You just couldn't put them through the pipeline fast enough, so we did it ourselves. Each company took a block of instruction and it was basically a five-week course. I'm sure it could have been better. But it was good enough and it focused on prep for combat, how to give an order, how to prep a unit to get out the door and do a mission, how to inspect them, how to do a post-mission critique and learn from what you did right, what you did wrong. You're teaching them the skills that you are going to demand they use when they get out there in a very challenging environment in Iraq.

We talked about language training. On my first deployment, Colonel Thomas C. Greenwood[1] got Defense Language Institute instructors from Monterey, California, to come to the battalion. We had about a sixty-day immersion course, thirty days in Camp Pendleton and then in the trans-Pacific. When you're on the ships, you've got nothing to do. We had about one hundred Marines at that time in language training, and then, when we got to Kuwait, the instructors went home, but we retained a fairly good training base.

What I changed the second time I deployed as a battalion commander is that I gave everybody the Defense Language Aptitude Battery, so we looked for people who had the propensity to learn languages. And then, like General McMaster said, I looked for people who just naturally had a gift of gab because we wanted to add those talkers in every squad throughout the battalion.

And so, with those two elements, we picked 150 Marines. They did a ninety-day immersion course because I had the contacts with the instructors from the previous deployment, brought them down to Camp Pendleton, and that's all these Marines did. They were Marines who already had a tour under their belt, so as far as going through the predeployment training program, again, with a five-month turnaround, I felt I could assume the risk of not putting them through it. I didn't ask anybody. And they didn't do anything but study language.

I was amazed at how quickly some of them picked up conversational Arabic. Could they write it? No. Could they read it? A little bit. But they could speak it enough to where they could act on it on the street. Everybody said this is a fight for information or intelligence. Well, if it is, you've got to talk to people to gain it. If you talk to them in their own language, they are much more receptive because they realize most Americans don't speak Arabic and they're kind of impressed when you do. It's one of those things to build rapport, which is the first key to starting up a relationship, and

---

[1] Commanding Officer, 15th Marine Expeditionary Unit. 1st Battalion, 1st Marines, was the Ground Combat Element of this expeditionary unit.

relationships mean everything in this culture. It really helped and I think it paid significant dividends. If you can, train even more Marines and for longer periods of time, because I think it is that important.

Cultural training was the same as every other unit. The basic infantry tactics, techniques, and procedures are important, but the tactics are not so complex. The decisions are complex, and that's what you focus on. You use your training always as a vehicle to put people—and test their decision making—through tactical decision games all the time so that you can do this.

You had to spend a lot of time training on intelligence collection because we don't routinely do it at the squad, platoon, and even battalion level. So, we looked at a process to do that. Here's how I organized to solve the problem, and I'll only talk about H and S [Headquarters and Service] Company—245 Marines: cooks, bakers, candlestick makers. I used them to reinforce my main effort. I formed provisional security platoons out of the company because most of its duties are life support for the battalion. But when you live on Camp Fallujah, you don't need any more life support. You've got more life support there than at Camp Pendleton.

So, I put these guys out in the fight and they loved it. Every Marine's a rifleman, they're doing fixed-site security so that my infantry Marines don't have to stand guard duty after an eight-hour patrol. They can either do mission prep or sleep, rest, do something else. It increased my ability to maneuver.

Rules of Engagement are a commander's issue, and I taught it. Now, the JAG [Judge Advocate General] was with me for any technical questions, but Marines don't like lawyers. They don't listen to them. And they don't want to be talked to by the guy who they think is a pencil-neck geek anyway. Most of your Marines didn't go to college. They don't understand lawyers, and they don't want to be told about a very critical part of their decision-making process—which is a law of armed conflict—by somebody they don't respect. They want to hear from their commanding officer. And so that's why I taught it. We reset every time we pulled platoons out to give them a shower and hot chow and retaught laws of armed conflict. And we went over vignettes of what we had either done well or not so well while we were executing the mission.

You have to remember that the hearts of your Marines will harden over time. If you don't understand that, you miss the point. These guys are on their third or fourth tours. They've seen buddies get killed and blown up.

They may have been blown up themselves and come back to duty. It's hard to tell them to like these people, but you have to talk to them about it in relevance to the mission and how treating them well and using the law of armed conflict benefits them as far as their legitimacy, as far as their ability to execute the mission, and actually saves fellow Marines' lives.

The big thing about combat leadership is supervise, supervise, supervise. You get out there. Once you're in the fight, you have to get out of that command post and go see every unit. I had, at one point, seven maneuver companies, thirty platoons. It took a week to see everybody face-to-face. When I talk about two levels down, I'm talking about looking the lieutenant in the eye, having him brief you on what he's doing. You know what he should be doing because you've given him the order, but you've got to go out there and see them actually do things.

The kinetics are easy. We get that. The nonkinetic civil affairs—PsyOps [Psychological Operations]—information operations working with civilian leaders, that's the hard part. I'm not saying going to guns is not important—and I think General McMaster said it well: "Don't ever lose a firefight, pursue every guy that's shooting until you got them." No one gets a free shot, is what I used to say. I don't care how far you've got to chase them. Chase them, run them down, and kill them if they choose to oppose you. But focus your efforts of your staff, the battalion, on the nonkinetic aspect of the fight.

Partnership—you've got to eat, live, and sleep with them to be effective.

The last point is if you remember nothing else, I would say—we all had signs that said it—Complacency Kills. And I told my Marines that that's really not true because it's the divine right of the PFC or lance corporal to be complacent. That's his right. He gets to do that. After he has his first firefight, he's going to be complacent. He's going to get comfortable in his environment, and it's his leadership that mitigates that natural phenomenon. If his leadership isn't caring, active, involved, he will be complacent and he will get himself killed because you didn't have the balls to do it right, get in his face, jack him up, and make sure he did it right.

Colonel William M. Jurney

The employment concept of military forces is first and foremost based on getting at the enemy. That's the perspective I come from in my battalion view regarding lessons and experiences from Ramadi between 2006 and 2007.

With an offensive mindset and not a defensive one, you look for and go after that which allows you to take and maintain the initiative against that which opposes you. There is no cookie-cutter solution or template for this. All too often, I think, that's what we see folks seeking, that there's got to be one set template approach. I would submit to you that that's just not going to be the case.

In counterinsurgency, however, you can expect the key terrain to be the population. So the question comes up as to whether you should be population focused or enemy focused. And I submit to you that the answer is "yes." You cannot look at one without understanding the full implications to the other.

The key thing that I said just now was "understanding," which is much different from assuming or misplacing your own Western bias onto the actions or reactions of particular events in a given area of operations. Wide variances can exist from one local area to the next. Therefore, you must account for and understand the specific nuances for each local area or community. From that point, you can already see that an effective tactical concept of employment, by necessity, is going to come predominantly from a bottom-up point of view.

In my framing of the population focus or enemy focus, I would submit that the population is viewed more as a means to get at the enemy versus a standalone end state. It's not that civil-military operations or civic action should not be aligned to meet the needs of the people. It's just that they have to be more closely aligned and prioritized by that which gives you the greatest tactical advantage against the enemy first.

Often, I've seen civil-military actions that are not connected to either the needs of the people or anything else that ties to improving a unit's ability to hurt the enemy. That's not meant to be a disparaging comment about our civil affairs efforts, but rather at the decisions of commanders, because it is a commander's decision, it's no different than ordering an attack. This brings me to my next point, which is that you cannot understand something that you do not live with, sleep with, and operate with every day and night. Effective counterinsurgency operations in and around populated centers require a permanent, persistent, credible security force. It cannot be part time. You will not gain the level of understanding of the situation, or the trust of the people, if you're not there 24/7.

The best security force is homegrown. It's local. Some might think that I'm simply advocating the last experience in Ramadi with the Awakening.[2] Actually, no. The Awakening was a growing movement that was making a difference outside the city of Ramadi in late 2006. And although it helped in providing new recruits for outside the city of Ramadi—which was a good thing—this movement and its recruits were from surrounding rural areas, and they would not operate within the city proper. Therefore, they were not the ideal local type that you want, who knows the streets and knows the people.

Yes, at some point we hoped that a national identification of governmental forces transcends a struggling country psyche, but near-term counterinsurgency is not going to happen. Make no mistake, the best security and sense of security for locals are local, and that local security force will also know the area and its people in such a way that no level of cultural understanding will ever bring.

A local security force is the enemy's worst nightmare. If the enemy loses his ability to hide in plain sight, then he loses his freedom of movement and action. He also loses the ability to replenish his own ranks with new recruits. So, you're hurting the enemy and you're meeting the essential needs within your area of operations for employment; money; prestige; honor; and even a sense of adventure for some by joining a legitimate government security force, which also allows, culturally speaking, a desired venue to prove yourself a man and a warrior.

Some will argue that a 24/7 combined action battalion concept for partnering an entire battalion and its leadership with newly forming security forces in the populated areas is simply too risky. I would not disagree more. I submit there's not only greater risk to the force but also an even greater risk to successful accomplishment of the mission if you choose to operate from some isolated, disconnected forward operating base while conducting

---

[2] Beginning in 2006, the al-Anbar Awakening, or *Sahawa al-Anbar*, was a revolt of Sunni tribes against al-Qaeda in the western Iraqi province of Anbar.

independent or intermittent partnered U.S. ops [operations] that lack permanent presence and a connection to the people.

Last, I suggest that our tactical concepts of employment must pursue multiple lines of effort concurrently if you're going to take the initiative. Kinetic and nonkinetic, regular and irregular, conventional and nonconventional—you pick the moniker of the day. There are many. However, focusing on the enemy by only pursuing U.S. targeted raids, all under the framework of "clear, hold, and build," is not enough to truly be on the offensive and take the initiative. They're essential and they're viable ops. But I would not suggest that such a narrow approach should be pursued.

I have seen time and again the limited activity of general purpose forces waiting on the big one to emerge for that game-changing targeted raid, to kill or capture an all important individual. This single line of effort is simply not going to work in gaining you the initiative, nor will it work for a unit that simply follows a lockstep, sequential approach along the clear-hold-build construct.

I suggest that in building or holding one might in fact clear the enemy without a firefight. If so, then why would you limit yourself to only those tools that we traditionally associate with conventional ops against a fixed enemy force, especially when you can't even find the enemy? Therefore, you should cast your net wide along all viable lines of effort if they can help you get at the enemy. Actions that you take should either directly or indirectly lead to improving our ability to impose our will on the enemy.

Discussions of civil-military ops, key leader engagement, training and employment of local security forces, restricting lines of movement, population control measures, census taking, improving governance and essential services, all are techniques and methods to be applied and/or combined as a leader sees fit based on a continuous process that sees a tactical advantage at taking up such actions. If not, then I submit that you're likely putting men and women at risk for nothing. Moreover, you could actually be making your own situation worse by inadvertently disenfranchising the most critical element of getting at the enemy: the population.

Colonel Julian Dale Alford

We three on the stage here have known each other as brothers for literally twenty years. Our families, our friends, we've spent many, many hours over the last twenty years drinking beer together and, on occasion, sipping a glass of whiskey talking about this stuff. And what I just heard over the last thirty minutes, I could say again over and over and expand on each of those points because we literally know what each other think. And that's a unique thing about the Marine Corps that you need to understand.

I'll address lessons from al-Qa'im and how they transfer to Afghanistan. I had an opportunity to command a battalion in Afghanistan in 2004, came home for seven months, went back to Iraq with the same battalion, literally the same battalion: the same five company commanders and three XOs [executive officers], that was a unique piece the 3d Battalion, 6th Marines, were able to do. And then this past year I spent nine months in Afghanistan working for a great soldier named General David McKiernan.

I will reiterate what Bill [Jurney] said: is it population-centric versus enemy-centric? Yes. Again, it's both. You can look at al-Qa'im and say we did Iron Fist—a battalion-size operation—and then a regimental-size operation, Steel Curtain, to take back the area.

That was a means to an end, though. As we moved and did that, we literally dropped off platoons to build positions and at the end of a ten-week period, we had fourteen. And we immediately moved the Iraqi Army in with us. I learned many of those things at the first tour in Afghanistan— mistakes made—and was able to use that the next year in Iraq.

How does that transition to Afghanistan? What I see there—and I had the opportunity to travel around the entire country, visit many, many units including our NATO [North Atlantic Treaty Organization] partners—is that we're completely an enemy-centric force.

We need to reposition a significant portion of our forward operating bases and combat outposts among the population because right now they're not. The problem is that they were built for counterterrorism missions in 2002 to 2004; they are in the wrong locations for a population-centric COIN [counterinsurgency] effort.

The second thing is that although we talk and write about it a lot, we are not focused on the Afghan Army, police, and border police. We don't live with them as partnered units. We consider partnering as link-up and do operations. If you're not sleeping with them, eating with them, and crapping in the same bucket, you're not partnered, and we're not partnered in Afghanistan.

Population-centric COIN is not about being nice to them, like Templer[3] said. His "hearts and minds" gets confused sometimes. It's about separating the population from the insurgents, protecting them, influencing them, and controlling the population, especially in the initial stages. We've talked already about the enemy. It's fluid. It hides in plain sight. The enemy does it.

What do we mean by "hearts and minds?" I think Dr. Mansoor brought up "trust and confidence." I totally agree. The heart or the trust is that we're in their best self-interests. We're in their best self-interest. The people have to believe that, and in their mind or their confidence in us they have to believe that we are going to win, and when I say "we," it's the Afghan Army and police with our support and their government. They have to believe that we're going to win and we're going to protect them. In their heart they have to believe we're in their best self-interest, and in their mind they believe that we are going to win. We're failing to do that.

If you're going to do population-centric COIN and you're going to live with the Afghan Army and police, how do you do that? The very first step is to understand who you're dealing with. This is based on my understanding of the Afghan people from my seventeen–eighteen months of experience in the country.

First, this is a quote I found and totally agree with: "They've learned to survive thirty years of war by hedging their bets." They've learned to play both sides. And they are still doing it. Why? Because they're getting slapped on one cheek by their government and the other cheek by the Taliban. They don't have a good choice, and we're not providing them a good choice because we're not population-centric, we're not among the people, and we're not with their army and police force. That's the first step. I was pleased to see General McChrystal's paper that he's written about it. Now we've got to execute it.

The next thing is that these people can read you better than any people I've ever been around, including my uncles who live in north Georgia, who

---

[3] Sir Gerald Templer, British High Commissioner in Malaya between 1952 and 1954 and commander of counterinsurgency efforts during the Malayan Emergency.

are very similar to them. They live off the land. They've learned over their lifetime, in order to survive, how to read people. You've got to understand that when you deal with them on a daily basis, if you're not sincere, they will see through you in a heartbeat and you will not be successful with them.

And the next point is about their problems. Their problem is they don't have honor and justice in their government. They believe their government is corrupt. Whether it is or not, they believe that. And they don't believe they have physical security, and a significant portion of the population doesn't have food security four or five months out of the year. Those three things, if we're among the people and with their army, we can focus on those. This is an important list.

The Afghans have based all their thoughts and decisions on history. When an Afghan looks at life, he looks backwards. He thinks about his history, he makes decisions off the oral history he knows of his society.

When we in the Western world look at life, we look forward. We think about how we're going to have a bigger house, better retirement, better car, and send my kid to college to get a better education.

When you deal with an Afghan, he makes decisions looking at life 180 degrees from the way you look at life. It's difficult for us to wrap our minds around and understand that. We must try to understand this better.

It's an agricultural-based society, which is extremely important, and much of their agriculture was destroyed in the past. We must focus our effort and our development to bring that back. But the first thing is we've got to be there among them.

And then there is the rural versus city dichotomy—80 percent of the population is a rural force. They don't want electricity in many of the homes. We think they do. Why did Iraqis want electricity? Because they had electricity. Many Afghans never had electricity. They want electricity to move water in their clinics and their schools, but in their homes, they're not begging for it, but we're trying in many cases to give it to them. We need to understand them better before we try to help them.

How do you get them to pick our side? This whole thing is about getting them to pick our side. Right now, they're playing defense. They're on defense because they're not picking our side. They don't believe in their hearts that we're in their best self-interest, and in their minds they don't know if we're going to win.

The Afghan culture is like the Iraqi culture on steroids. It's a weird mix between Pashtunwali and Islam, which in many cases are opposed to each other. And the parts where the insurgency really is, the east and the south—because this is a Pashtun insurgency, make no mistake about it— Pashtunwali is extremely strong even though something similar to it exists throughout the rest of the country. And it is a great code. It is very similar to the code that my uncles in north Georgia live by.

Understanding the people and their culture—you need to do that because that's all they have. That village elder who you deal with on a daily basis, if you're doing this business right, his honor and his culture and his history are all he has in life and he will kill you for it.

With the Afghan Army, you've got to leverage a culture. The leadership we've already talked about. The logistics of their force are weak and we had to work on that. You've got to accept chaos when you deal with the Afghan Army because it's going to be there. You've got to show that you're committed and risked your life right beside them. If you don't do that, they will not fight with you.

The army is an extremely credible force, especially at the company level and below. At the battalion and above, they're struggling, because they're trying to build the airplane while they fly it. And if we're with them all the time, which we're not now, as a partnered force, we can make that a lot better. Advisors and mentors are not enough. We have to evolve for that. We have to start with a partnered force and evolve to mentors and advisors and then work our way out of a job. We've got it backwards, I believe.

The Afghan police—there's got to be a local-based police, as Colonel Jurney talked about—they must be from the local area and the people have to know who they are. That's where the intelligence comes from and I believe that we, as a general purpose force, have to live with the police force.

I can do some math for you really quickly. Let's just say there are 360 districts. There are 388 but we'll say 360. I think an infantry battalion can do about twelve districts, and we've got some examples of this down south with the Marines in Delaram. That means thirty battalions or ten brigades. We've got to do some real math and tell some real truth about what it's going to take if we're going to do a population-centric COIN, because standing up the police is the most important thing we're doing and right now we're not focused on it.

The clusters in those districts, you'd be amazed at what happens when the Marines or soldiers live with them. The governor, the district governor moves and puts his house right by the police station. The district police chief moves right by the police station and stays there 24/7. The judge moves there. He can move the district support teams out of PRTs [Provincial Reconstruction Teams] into those areas. It becomes a cluster in those districts and that's where it matters in Afghanistan, down at the district level. We're failing to do that.

The last piece is the Afghan Border Police, the forgotten soldiers. They are a paramilitary fighting force. If you want to get into a firefight in Afghanistan, you partner with the Afghan Border Police. You'll get all the fighting you want. We're not doing it. And we must change the way we're doing it and we must do some real math on what it's going to take if we want to make a viable, stable Afghan country that no longer harbors terrorists. If that's so, then there are some hard lessons, some hard decisions that have to be made about what it's going to take.

Bing West

Colonel Alford and Colonel Jurney just said that the Afghan population doesn't know if we're going to win. There is no more devastating statement that could be made than that after we've been there for eight years.

As I listened, I went down the list of the recommendations versus what we're doing and it struck me between the eyes that the reason we're not doing any one of them is that risk aversion has now become so much part of our culture that I'm not persuaded we can make the changes. The risk aversion obviously starts right at the top and permeates our entire society.

Are we willing to have the casualties that it takes to turn things around? And the recommendations were, first, you need 24/7 patrolling in the populated areas. Right now we average one patrol per platoon per day for six out of the seven days. A platoon is about the smallest size that we're sending out with the MRAPs, etc., and we're tied to them to have water. So, if you do the math, we're showing up in any of the populated places for about thirty minutes a day. There's a big difference between being visible thirty minutes a day and being invisible for the rest of the day.

The second point was everyone said you have to be unremitting and finish the firefights. We're not finishing any firefights.

The third one was we need the Combined Action Program concept. Colonel Jurney said that the local security forces are the enemy's worst nightmare, and they sure are. No battalion out there today is permitted to go and recruit local forces the way we did in Vietnam and with the Sons of Iraq. This Combined Security Transition Command–Afghanistan organization is a little bit batty, but it controls things and we're doing everything from the top down according to a certain schedule, but the individual battalion isn't allowed to go out and do what Colonels Jurney, Alford, and Furness did so successfully in Iraq. I have seen combined action platoons pulled out by brigade commanders because they are too risky, when they had a platoon overnight somewhere, leaving the Embedded Training Teams [ETTs] there with the Afghans, the exact opposite of what we should be doing.

And finally, the notion of living with the Afghans, with the exception of the ETTs, and the British Operational Mentoring and Liaison Teams and our advisor teams, that's really just not being done today. So the gap between what the battalion commanders recommend and what we're doing couldn't be larger.

Part IV
Officer Development in the U.S. Military

Chapter 7

Officer Development for Counterinsurgency

by Nathaniel C. Fick

My platoon deployed in August 2001 as part of Battalion Landing Team, 1st Battalion, 1st Marines, on what we expected to be a routine western Pacific cruise. Piled high on the empty bunk in my stateroom were surfboards, guitars, and golf clubs—all the tools we thought we'd need for our six months in Asia and the Middle East.

Less than two years later, after serving in Afghanistan and Pakistan, many of these same Marines joined in the initial invasion of Iraq. Two incidents near Baghdad in the spring of 2003—barely eighteen months after the 9/11 attacks—shaped my views on counterinsurgency (COIN) leadership.

In early April, while on a mounted patrol in a small town, we had a single rocket-propelled grenade (RPG) round fired past our lead vehicle. I gave the order to do what I thought was tactically correct: dismount, sweep through the small collection of buildings, and find our shooter. Within minutes, we had rounded up the "military-age men" and lined them up facedown in the dirt, found most of the women and children huddled together in a single room, and concluded that whoever fired the RPG had long since disappeared into the adjacent palm grove. As we drove out of the village, I couldn't help thinking we'd done more harm than good.

A few weeks later, in a different village outside Baghdad, we were walking a foot patrol when I detected a hostility I hadn't felt before. Through an interpreter, I asked an Iraqi man what was wrong.

"Your sunglasses," he replied.

I and most of the Marines wore dark glasses in the midday glare.

"What about them?" I asked, assuming that he was offended by the inability to see our eyes.

"We think they are x-ray glasses and you are looking at our women."

This wasn't the answer I'd expected, so I took off my glasses and slipped them onto the Iraqi.

"Turn them on."

Faced with this seemingly intractable problem, we all took off our glasses and put them on the kids who invariably followed us around small towns. We continued the patrol, and immediately noticed that goodwill had returned.

The lesson, for me, was that these two events, each replicated thousands of times over many years of war, led to very different places.

Mark Moyar, in *A Question of Command: Counterinsurgency from the Civil War to Iraq,* identifies three schools of COIN thinking: enemy-centric, population-centric, and what he calls leader-centric. My first example, of sweeping through a village to find a shooter, is clearly enemy-centric, and the second, of removing our glasses to assuage local concerns, is more population-centric. There's actually a place for both, and the objective of good leader-centric training is to create decision makers who can strike the proper balance between fighting the enemy and protecting the people.

In seeking to define a good leader-centric process, Moyar lists ten attributes of effective COIN leaders: initiative, flexibility, creativity, judgment, empathy, charisma, sociability, dedication, integrity, and organization. Compare his list to the fourteen Marine Corps Leadership

Traits, known by the mnemonic JJ DID TIE BUCKLE: justice, judgment, dependability, initiative, decisiveness, tact, integrity, enthusiasm, bearing, unselfishness, courage, knowledge, loyalty, and endurance.

Three are exactly the same: initiative, judgment, and integrity. Many of the rest are fairly close in meaning: dedication versus endurance, tact versus sociability. But there exists one glaring gap between them: where Moyar highlights flexibility and creativity, the Marine Corps list makes no mention of these attributes or anything like them.

This is not to imply that the Marine Corps doesn't value flexibility and creativity. In previous generations, the Corps pioneered amphibious assault, vertical envelopment, and combined-arms operations. But there is a difference between a force that is creative and flexible in its doctrine, and a force that recognizes, values, and rewards flexibility and creativity among its junior leaders. In fact, it is the latter which makes the former possible.

Secretary of Defense Robert M. Gates has said, "In the end, the military capabilities we need cannot be separated from the cultural traits and reward structure of the institutions we have: the signals sent by what gets funded, who gets promoted, what is taught in the academies and staff colleges, and how we train." His fiscal year 2010 budget proposal signaled the first major move to "rebalance" the Department of Defense's programs to enhance our ability to fight today's wars and to succeed in the operations we are most likely to face in the years ahead, while also hedging against other risks and contingencies. This approach is similar to that of any tactical commander who prepares for the enemy's most likely course of action, while also hedging against his most dangerous course of action.

Balancing risk must transcend weapon acquisition programs—important as they are—and permeate the philosophy of training, educating, and retaining military leaders. At least as important as developing a clear vision of the capabilities of future enemies is developing an officer corps capable of combating and adapting to the unforeseen enemy. We don't have the luxury of one known future, but must prepare for many possible futures. There will not be one type of future war; our enemies will continuously adapt to avoid our surfaces and exploit our gaps. Leaders must therefore have the agility to anticipate and rapidly react to a wide variety of situations. Instead of training all officers for all reasonably foreseeable threats—perhaps a viable strategy during the Cold War, but an impossible one in the threat environment we face today—we must develop a cadre of officers capable of adapting to situations for which they have not been trained and prepared, while doing all that we can to prepare them for the most likely situation they will face: persistent conflict by hybrid enemies employing asymmetrical strategies and tactics.

This does not require a major break with the past. The basic principles of combat—shoot, move, and communicate—and the bedrock principles articulated in MCDP 1, *Warfighting*, still apply. But we may benefit from examining several aspects of our officer accession and training process.

I graduated from a small liberal arts college in New England where exposure to the military was fairly limited. I then went on to serve with many service academy graduates, and had the opportunity to watch my sister and brother-in-law work their way through the Naval Academy while I was still on active duty. In my earliest days at The Basic School (TBS), as a newly commissioned second lieutenant, it seemed to me that the service academy graduates had advantages that I would never match: they spoke the language of the military, knew the rules of the strange game we were all playing, and seemed to have friends everywhere. I, on the other hand, kept confusing hatches with bulkheads.

But that playing field leveled very, very quickly. By the time we had graduated from TBS, we were essentially peers. And by the time we'd spent six months or a year in Fleet units, people's reputations rose and fell according to their abilities rather than their commissioning source.

In my experience, the training that really matters is what happens in the operational units. That's where the culture is shaped, and that's where the most realistic and memorable training occurs. So, I'd like to focus on three very simple concepts, getting back to my earlier assertion that the fundamental tenets still apply, and that preparing for twenty-first-century warfare does not require a break with all that's come before: the three-block war, the strategic corporal, and tactical ethics.

The three-block war is an organizing construct that values adaptation, that values training leaders with the mental agility to shift seamlessly from combat in one city block to keeping an uneasy peace in a second block, to providing humanitarian support in the third. Leaders must play by the right rules in the right block, avoiding the sort of lax conduct that led to the killing of a Marine on Failaka Island in 2002 (resulting in the inauguration of General James N. Mattis's "guardian angel" concept), but also avoiding the kind of amped-up overreactions that contributed to the killings in Haditha.

This leads naturally to the idea of the strategic corporal, the notion that a private in today's military can have an impact far greater than a private in Napoleon's army. Indeed, the actions of an individual Marine or soldier can have repercussions internationally. This is a result of several trends: increasingly lethal weapons, the emergence of a twenty-four-hour global media, and the distribution of operations enabled by communications and transportation technology (to such an extent that junior leaders are routinely expected to act without orders). Recall the advice found hanging on a company commander's plywood door in southwest Baghdad: "In the absence of orders or guidance, figure out what they should have been and execute vigorously."

If we as a military and as a nation are going to trust our strategic corporals to execute vigorously, to do the right thing, and to be truly empowered leaders making independent decisions on which much rides, then we simply must better integrate our tactical ethics training into the normal training of operational units. Our warrior culture must embrace the same passionate intolerance for unlawful and immoral acts on the battlefield that it currently has for leaving a comrade behind, and also embrace the fact that our junior leaders have a continuous and never-ending duty to make this so.

When young Americans join our ground forces—the Marine and Army combat arms, and the Special Operations Forces—they seek to join what General David H. Petraeus calls "the brotherhood of the close fight." They want to be part of the pack. Most—and I know I was in this category—have visions of glory and gunfights, not patience and proportionality. In the heat of the fight, when people are dying, it can be tempting to dismiss ethical considerations as a distant, and lesser, concern. That is wrong. Sound ethical conduct is absolutely essential to both mission accomplishment and troop welfare.

Polls consistently show that the military is the most trusted institution in American life—more than the police, the church, and even the Supreme Court. Maintaining that trust is a sacred obligation that helps to ensure the public support that our warriors need to accomplish the mission, to win. Now, in terms of troop welfare, every war eventually ends, and then the warriors revert to private citizens again. They go on with their lives. Their leaders have a duty to do everything possible to ensure that they can look their children and grandchildren in the eye, and at themselves in the mirror, when talking about their service in wartime.

I'm one of those people now—a former junior officer leading a civilian organization in a competitive industry and trying each day to adapt and stay ahead and apply the lessons I learned in the Marines. I'd like to highlight three of the lessons here, in the expectation that they apply more or less equally in warfare and in business.

First, there's a difference between legal authority and moral authority. The military is pretty simple in the sense that each member wears his rank on his collar and his resume on his chest. When a new second lieutenant checks into his first unit, that rank—the gold bar on his collar—actually means something. There's all sorts of history and institutional authority vested in it. That formal authority, however, lasts about five minutes in conversation, and about five seconds in a firefight. What really matters is moral, or informal, authority. I saw moral authority accrue to people who did two things: they were technically and tactically proficient, and they genuinely cared for the welfare of the people in their charge. Moral authority and rank aren't necessarily correlated, and so hierarchical organizations must have a feedback mechanism to allow the views of junior people with high moral authority to be heard, both because those views can improve the organization as a whole, and because those individuals will tend to leave if they feel that their input isn't having any effect on the organization.

Second, diversity of experience matters. Modern warfare is a lot more complicated than a bayonet charge, and leaders are more likely to recognize problems and adapt quickly to meet them when they have been exposed to a wide range of situations and have had to work with widely differing groups. To that end, the military would benefit from more career on-ramps and off-ramps, from sabbatical years for education or work experience in other sectors, and even from increased lateral-entry options for people with important skill sets. Such a shift in personnel policies would have two beneficial effects: easing the recruitment and retention of more good people, and increasing the quality of people across the force.

Third, people must be allowed to fail. They must be allowed to fail not only to encourage them to be bold, and not only to allow them to learn, but also—paradoxically—because allowing them to fail makes it easier for commanders to fail them. I'm thinking specifically of relief. In today's military, relief of command is equivalent to public humiliation and the end of an officer's career. In the past—as recently as just before the war in Vietnam—relief could simply be the recognition that a particular commander was not the right person for this specific job at this particular time. It was not unusual for commanders to be relieved of one command and then to go on and perform at a high level in another assignment. By equating relief with execution, our system has the perverse effect of keeping the wrong people in the wrong jobs for too long. Modern warfare, with its staggering array of tasks, demands a more flexible and resilient system.

Saint Augustine reminds us that the only purpose for war is to create a better peace. In every phase of combat our leaders must constantly keep that better peace in mind. We don't have the luxury of one future, and so must train for many possible futures. The twenty-first-century officer must be able to transition rapidly across the spectrum of operations—from offense to defense to stability and support operations. These may all occur simultaneously, and the transition from one to the other will often be made at the discretion of junior leaders—with huge ramifications for the United States and our standing in the world. The nation needs smart and well-trained military leaders who can adapt to new circumstances while remaining true to their bedrock principles—strategic corporals in the three-block war.

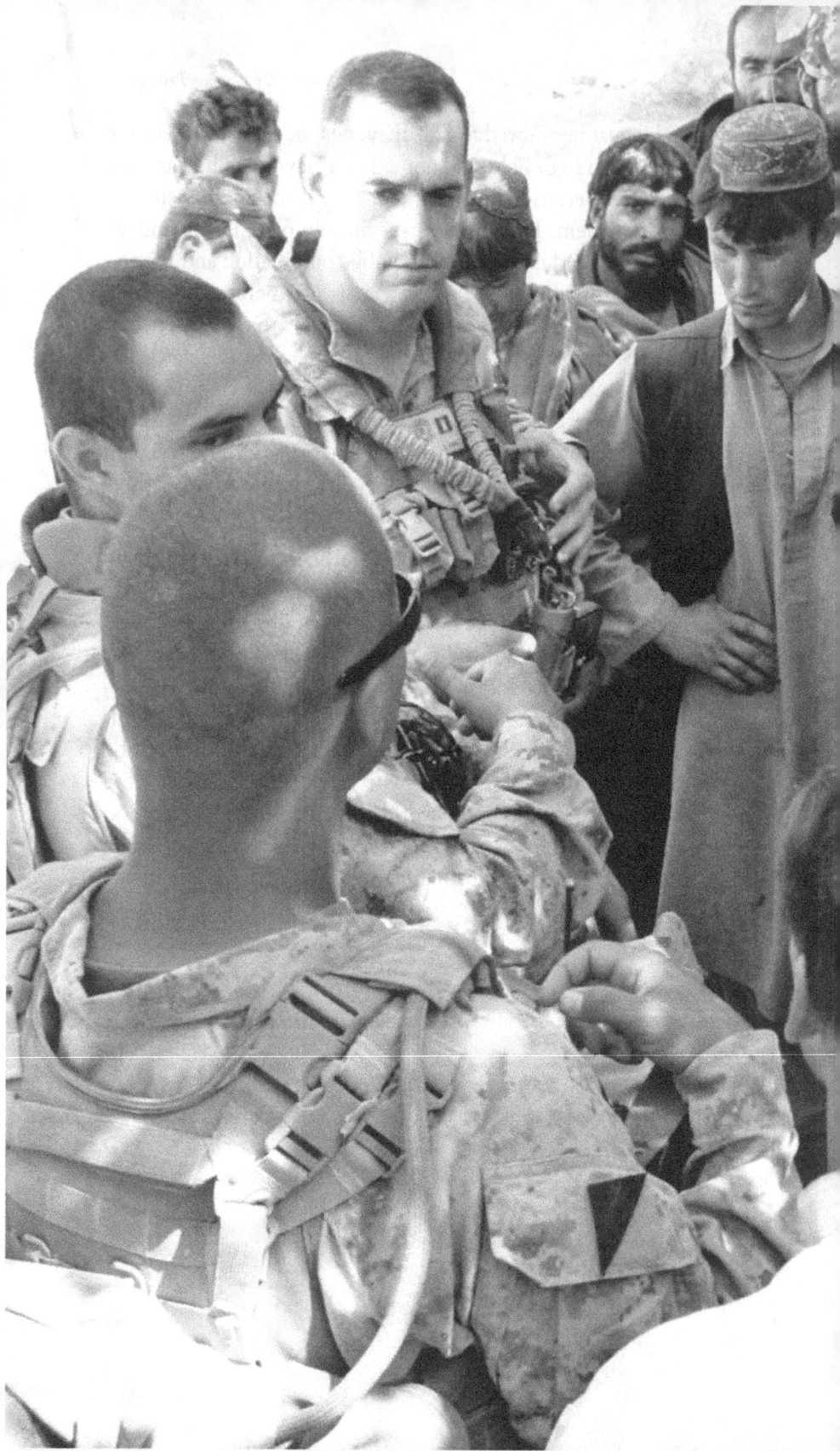

Chapter 8

The "Major" Challenge of Junior Officer Leadership Development and Talent Management

by Paula D. Broadwell

The key to many of our successes in Iraq, in fact, has been leaders—especially young leaders—who have risen to the occasion and taken on tasks for which they'd had little or no training, and who have demonstrated enormous initiative, innova-tiveness, determination, and courage.

—*General David H. Petraeus*[1]

As Mark Moyar states in his book *A Question of Command: Counterinsurgency from the Civil War to Iraq*, "Regardless of how brilliant or dynamic the national and intermediate [counterinsurgency] leaders are, they do not achieve success in counterinsurgency when their local [or

---

[1] LtGen David H. Petraeus, USA, "Learning Counterinsurgency: Observations from Soldiering in Iraq," *Military Review*, January–February 2006, 52.

junior] commanders are devoid of leadership abilities."[2] Decentralization—the distribution and delegation of responsibilities to lower-ranking individuals—is not a new phenomena on the battlefield. As Moyar notes, "Decentralized command has, in fact, been the hallmark of effective counterinsurgency since ancient times, except in the case where insurgents meet large conventional forces."[3] The acknowledged prevalence since 9/11 of counterinsurgency (COIN) operations demands a flattened battlefield hierarchy, and a particular emphasis on junior officer leadership development. This demand, however, is contrary to existing military hierarchical authority and management principles. Concurrently, most junior officers are not trained to assume or understand the totality of needs and responsibilities at their level, nor do they all have the experience to appropriately apply the tools if they did. Additionally, many of their superiors are inherently risk averse and may be leery about permitting a forward-based junior officer the leeway that COIN may require. All of these conditions lead to this basic question: are we employing junior officers in the best manner possible?

Given the increasingly decisive role that junior officers play on the frontlines, U.S. Army leaders have placed renewed emphasis on reviewing the allocation of tasks to this body of soldiers, as well as on examining the quality and readiness of the force. In this chapter, I first examine the allocation of tasks to junior officers and expand upon the benefits and pitfalls of their crucible experiences. Second, I highlight critical talent retention issues, illustrating the Army's "quick-fix" approaches and exploring the root causes behind the shortfall. Finally, I advocate for a stronger enterprise talent management as a long-term approach to preserving the health and effectiveness of the U.S. Army junior officer corps.

Allocating Leadership Tasks to Junior Officers

The decentralized nature of the COIN fight demands that we give maximum responsibility to the smallest units, according to battle-seasoned officers of all ranks. Indeed, a brigade or battalion commander cannot

---

[2] Mark Moyar, *A Question of Command: Counterinsurgency from the Civil War to Iraq* (New Haven: Yale University Press, 2009), 6.

[3] Ibid., 5.

supervise every aspect of COIN. The nature of today's wars requires that national and intermediate leaders provide clear intent and meaningful guidance, and show trust in the most junior officers to prepare them to make decisions and lead their units within effective frameworks. "No battalion in this fight could succeed if junior officers could not be trusted with the most difficult and sensitive of missions," comments Major Chuck Rush.[4]

With this tall order, junior Army officer leaders need a new mix of competencies to meet with personal success and to effectively prepare their own subordinates for the contemporary operating environment and the uncertainty that lies beyond. We must also adequately train and equip them to operate in full-spectrum environments replete with kinetic threats and nonkinetic enablers. The confluence of the many uncertain variables associated with the Army's projected threat environment—globalization, technological advances, demographic changes, urbanization, resource demand, climate change and natural disasters, proliferation of weapons of mass destruction, and failed or failing states—requires us to think deeply and broadly in our leadership development programs.[5] In doing so, we must also acknowledge the distribution of skills that different officers bring to the battlefield, and we must strive to ensure adequate junior officer leadership development and talent management.

Unquestionably, our soldiers have faced diverse leadership tasks and challenges since the inception of the armed forces. Indeed, the threats to our national security have often changed, and so have the paradigms within which our military organizes to train and prepare to meet the threats. Through those lenses, there is nothing new under the sun. What has changed is the breadth of tasks that we are asking our volunteer force to accomplish—often without adequate training, education, or experience.

Pentathlete Officers

Fortunately, senior Army leaders are taking strides to cope with the diversity of challenges inherent in COIN, peacekeeping, and stability operations. In response to operations in Iraq and Afghanistan, the Army

---

[4] Maj Chuck Rush, USA, email interview with author, 18 September 2009.

[5] Draft of Chief of Staff of the Army white paper, received via email at Harvard University on 11 July 2007.

has expanded its normative leadership development vision to that of developing multiskilled, adaptable, and flexible modern-day pentathletes. The *pentathlete* is a superb individual athlete who competes in very diverse and demanding athletic events. Similarly, Army officers need to possess the same breadth of talents for the military profession: unquestioned strength in their Army core competency; professional adaptability and flexibility; and expertise in nontraditional areas such as multicultural, interagency, and intergovernmental settings. All these important characteristics are the goals of the Army's pentathlete vision.[6]

The Army Chief of Staff's new vision reflects the leadership tasks that our junior leaders have faced in the last eight years. First, the vision expects the individual to be a competent warfighter—tactically, technically, and technologically proficient. These individuals must possess negotiation skills and understand the nuances of serving as interlocutors for unsavory characters when required by our rules of engagement (ROE) to protect these characters, even when this is much to their disdain. On a micro level, the leaders must possess strong interpersonal skills—such as empathy, charisma, sociability—for building human relations and strong teams. They must be self-starters and initiative takers.

Junior officers must be managers of change in large organizations and understand how their organization synergizes with the collective effort. They must possess cognitive skills in math and economics, and have the ability to communicate persuasively in oral and written form. They must possess broad problem-solving frameworks that will brand them as strategic and creative thinkers. We also expect them to self-develop language and cultural skills. Further, they must be confident in their decision making (even if it is only 80 percent right) and competencies, and they must be willing to place duty, honor, and country above themselves.

Crucible Experiences

Our junior officers engulfed in these myriad tasks in Iraq and Afghanistan face both an opportunity and a test. The environment is one

---

[6] Col Jesse Farrington, USA, "Army Developing Strategic Leaders while Maintaining the Warfighting Edge," 30 March 2007, http://www.dtic.mil/cgi-bin/GetTRDoc?AD=ADA467210&Location= U2&doc=GetTRDoc.pdf (1 November 2009).

of joint, combined, civil-military, multinational players. In this high-profile arena, many of our junior leaders have faced a *crucible experience*—a test of "place, time, or situation characterized by the confluence of powerful intellectual, social, economic, or political forces."[7] Their role on the frontline provides the opportunity to influence global affairs and gain valued leadership experience—skills invaluable to the military and to the private sector.

Concomitantly, this crucible experience is a test of their fortitude and resilience. According to well-known leadership author Warren G. Bennis, such an experience "is a defining moment that unleashes abilities, forces crucial choices, and sharpens focus. It teaches a person who he or she is."[8]

These defining environments in Operation Iraqi Freedom and the International Security Assistance Force are forcing our junior leaders to confront the hard realities of complex situations—such as relatively restrictive ROE, and the presence of innocents on the battlefield—with their need to accomplish the mission. In a shift from the days of a less-professional conscript force, we hold our junior officers more accountable for recognizing the strategic implications of their actions in a complex moral environment. Indeed, their choices in "gray area" decision-making dilemmas (e.g., treatment of detainees) can have global repercussions. As one astute lieutenant in a 2007 War College survey conducted by retired Army Lieutenant Colonel Leonard Wong at the Strategic Studies Institute (SSI) noted, "The fact is that we do not lower our standards and we abide by a ROE; that we are not out there just to kill innocent civilians; and that the mission is important, but the means to that end is sometimes more important."[9] Such words speak volumes about how adept our junior officers are becoming in dealing with the moral complexities in their post-9/11 crucible experiences.

The diversity of mental, physical, and psychological tasks that our junior officers accomplish in the contemporary operating environment is immense.

---

[7] *American Heritage Dictionary* quoted in Warren G. Bennis and Robert J. Thomas, *Geeks & Geezers: How Era, Values, and Defining Moments Shape Leaders* (Boston: Harvard Business School Press, 2002), 14.

[8] Bennis and Thomas, *Geeks & Geezers*, 16.

[9] LtCol Leonard Wong, USA (Ret), "Developing Adaptive Leaders: The Crucible Experience of Operation Iraqi Freedom," July 2004, http://www.strategicstudiesinstitute.army.mil/pubs/display.cfm?pubID=411 (accessed 15 September 2009). Special thanks to LtCol Wong and this study for insights provided from junior officers.

Our future leaders must expect complexity and understand that they will often have to operate autonomously, often without clear intent or guidance. In this environment, they engage in tactical fights. They support host-nation community development missions. They oversee the application of Commander's Emergency Response Program funds at will and run controversial Psychological Operations missions. They equip and train foreign security forces that may wear flip-flops to work. They negotiate with local leaders in matters of great strategic political importance. They are diplomats and public spokespersons with the media. They build universities and manage sewage and utility stations. They serve as "strategic lieutenants," placed in high-level Iraqi or Afghan host-nation ministerial offices, and they are responsible for engaging with key indigenous leaders as liaisons for U.S. commanding generals. Unquestionably, a twentysomething soldier can and does influence world politics.

Faucet Phenomenon

Beyond these tasks, junior officers must wrestle with another responsibility—the stress and strains of constant combat. The psychological aspects of COIN have presented junior officers with what many of them call the faucet phenomenon: the necessity of adjusting to situations that could change from cold to hot and back to cold instantaneously.[10] In one morning, a junior leader may be handing out pens and paper to Iraqi children, and then have to face the moral dilemma of shooting a pregnant woman who has voluntarily positioned herself as a human shield in front of hidden insurgents. An officer on patrol with his troops may be immersed in the horrific surrealism of thirty mutilated bodies dismembered by a vehicle-borne improvised explosive device, then return to his base quarters to hang out with friends and Skype with his children back home. He may be in a high-adrenaline gunfight in one moment, then have to calm himself and his troops to go knocking on doors in various neighborhoods to "win hearts and minds" while seeking the gunfight's instigators. This is a remarkably broad expectation of tactical, moral, ethical, and psychological duties for officers with little frontline experience, and many with no training or education in COIN.

---

[10] Ibid., 5.

An interesting paradox arises in this COIN environment. More junior officers are gaining invaluable leadership experience on the frontlines. In aggregate, we are developing a larger corps of seasoned officers. Many of these individuals have illustrated their ability to adapt and overcome professional challenges, especially those with prior world travel and out-of-the-box formative experiences (such as study abroad during college or civilian graduate school as a midcareer officer). However, when the SSI study probed junior officers about their experiences, asking them if their Iraq tour made them more proficient in their particular branch, most officers (except for infantrymen) responded that they felt they were not gaining proficiency. Their experiences highlight a COIN paradox: gaining experience but losing branch proficiencies. Tankers are dismounting (a cardinal sin); artillerymen are patrolling the streets; and female cooks, military police, or aviators are serving on "female engagement teams" in direct support of combat units—and against Department of Defense (DoD) combat exclusion policies. But in spite of the loss of technical skills or circumvention of military policies, many respondents highlighted that they were becoming better officers in general and better leaders specifically. The paradox, therefore, stems from the reality that while they are gaining experience and building on a critical pillar of leader development, many officers are losing branch-specific skills to the detriment of force preparedness for a conventional or total-war scenario.

A quote from Mark Twain, musing in his book *Life on the Mississippi*, sums up officers' task-oriented and psychological challenges precisely: "Two things seemed pretty apparent to me. One was, that in order to be a [Mississippi River] pilot, a man has got to learn more than any one man ought to be allowed to know; and the other was, that he must learn it all over again in a different way every 24 hours."

While the adaptive "pentathlete officer" goal is the normative expectation, there are inherent additional ramifications for the individual when we begin to ask too much. Post-traumatic stress disorder has stricken some officers. In addition, the Army soldier suicide rate was the highest in its history this year. The mental and emotional strains placed on some young leaders who see no end in sight to our operations may question how much longer they and, perhaps even more so, their families can pay the price of their separation. According to a Pentagon survey in early 2009, "more than 40 percent of military members are parents," a higher percentage than ever before, and "more than 230,000 children have parents serving in Iraq or Afghanistan."[11] Children invariably feel the strains of an absent, wounded, or deceased parent, and so do spouses. In fact, according to DoD, divorce rates have increased since 9/11 in both the Army and the Marines at a faster pace than our societal rate. Although officers generally suffer at lower rates than enlisted soldiers in these personal issues, they are not immune. The confluence of these many sociological and psychological challenges places great strains on the readiness of our force and are a cause of retention problems.

Retention Issues

With these strains on our force so evident, it is no wonder that senior military leaders are reflecting on our next course of action in this operating environment. A recent *Foreign Policy* article titled "General Casey's Doubts"[12] describes the Army's highest ranking officer's views on officer retention and the rarely discussed strategic risks inherent in an Afghanistan troop surge. According to the article, General George W. Casey Jr. fears that the size and duration of this commitment could eventually break the all-volunteer Army. He is specifically concerned about junior officers.

Why is there a critical shortage of majors during a period of growth for the Army, what is the cause, and how is the Army addressing the challenge?

The Army Chief of Staff has openly acknowledged that we are already at a critical juncture with the health of the junior officer corps. In fact, the Army is about 15 percent short of its goal of 15,700 majors, as Figure 1 illustrates.

The Army is no longer hemorrhaging junior officers, due in part to the state of the economy and incentives such as the G.I. Bill. In the last year, the lack of mid-career civilian jobs and levels of unemployment have served as deterrents to jumping ship. However, the underlying bad news is that the junior officer supply is only holding steady at a rate that is 15 to 20 percent under required strength and there is no comprehensive Army strategy to eliminate the shortfall.

---

[11] Robert Gates, "Joint Armed Forces Officers' Wives' Luncheon" (speech given by Secretary of Defense, Bolling Air Force Base, MD, 26 June 2009). Available: http://www.defenselink.mil/speeches/speech.aspx?speechid=1364 (accessed 28 October 2009).

[12] Robert Haddick, "General Casey's Doubts," *Foreign Policy*, 23 October 2009.

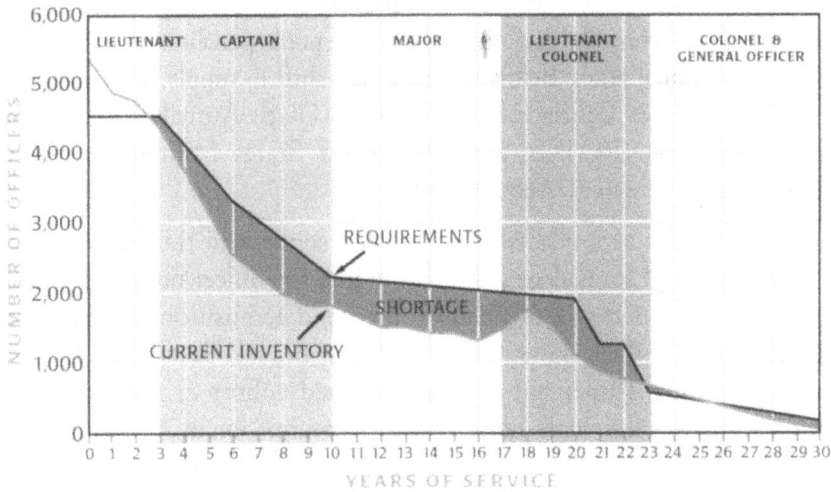

Figure 1. U.S. ARMY PERSONNEL REQUIREMENTS AND INVENTORY

Data are from the Total Army Personnel Database as of September 2007 and the Manning Authorization Document as of September 2007. Chart extracted from the April 2009 SSI Report.[13]

Quick Fixes to the Officer Shortage

A 2007 U.S. Government Accountability Office (GAO) Retention Report stated that the Army projects a shortage of 3,000 or more officers annually through Fiscal Year 2013.[14] To address the 20 percent shortcoming in officer strength across the junior ranks, the Army has implemented a zealous promotion rate for eligible lieutenants (from 60 percent in 1997 to 90 percent in 2008). Furthermore, 97 percent of eligible captains, and 95 percent of eligible majors will be promoted this year. All of these factors have had a cascading effect on the overall force quality as young officers do not have the time in key jobs to master their duties and responsibilities. Needless to say, there is little culling going on within these ranks.

---

[13] Col Casey Wardynski, Maj David S. Lyle, and LtCol Michael J. Colarusso (Ret), USA, "Towards a U.S. Army Officer Corps Strategy for Success: A Proposed Human Capital Model Focused upon Talent," April 2009, http://www.strategicstudiesinstitute.army.mil/pubs/display.cfm?PubID=912 (accessed 13 September 2009), 3.

[14] For additional information, see the GAO report to the Committee on Armed Services, House of Representatives, titled "Military Personnel: Strategic Plan Needed to Address Army's Emerging Officer Accession and Retention Challenges" (January 2007, GAO-07-224).

In addition to these accelerated promotion rates, we have developed another quick fix by shifting our recruitment pools percentages within the traditional source pools. Below is a list of the shift in supply rates from the three main sources: Officer Candidate School (OCS), Army Reserve Officer Training Corps (ROTC), and the United States Military Academy (USMA; also known as West Point).[15]

OCS serves as a pathway for enlisted soldiers to transition to the officer corps and for college graduates to join the officer ranks. The OCS route was designed as a mechanism for rapid acquisition of officers in response to mobilization requirements. Over the last decade, OCS grew from providing 10 percent of commissioned cohort to more than 40 percent, and was the single largest source of commission in 2008, according to Office of Economic and Manpower Analysis (OEMA).

Army ROTC traditionally provides the bulk of new officers through its two- to four-year scholarship programs. Candidates go through a combination of military science training in conjunction with regular college education at approximately 270 colleges across the United States. ROTC provides each service with the flexibility to adjust the number of graduates who are commissioned into either the Active or Reserve components each year to meet changing manpower objectives. It has historically provided nearly 70 percent of the annual cohort, but there has been a steady decline since the late 1990s. ROTC now provides around 42 percent or 2,100 officers annually, according to the OEMA. In 2006, ROTC was nearly 6,000 candidates short of its goal. The Army has filled the lacuna with commissions from OCS.

The shift in commissions from ROTC to OCS requires the Army to reach deeper into its pool of seasoned sergeants to commission new officers. The consequence is that the quality of the share of OCS candidates is decreasing, as evidenced by their scores on the Armed Forces Qualification Test—a test that determines basic qualification for enlistment and predicts future aptitude and career success. Put another way, in OEMA's words, to fill our ranks we are commissioning "officers with a reduced likelihood of academic or occupational success" at a pace faster than ever before. Finally,

---

[15] A fourth source of commissions comes from direct commissions (DCs). DCs serve the professional branches of the Army (the Army Medical Department, the Judge Advocate General's Corps, and the Army Chaplain Corps) and provide civilian-degreed leaders a means to receive a commission in their career field. For commissioning sources, see http://www.goarmy.com/officer.

by granting commissions to senior NCOs who are already near their retirement mark, the Army indeed gains a seasoned veteran but he or she will remain on active duty at lower rates than all other commissioned scholarship officers, so this ultimately does not help make up for the dearth of high-quality officers.

The USMA provides a congressionally mandated 20 percent of commissions or approximately 950 candidates each year (of an applicant pool of nearly 13,000). These numbers have remained steady over the decades, and thankfully, the quality selection pool (based on applicant grade point average, leadership endeavors, athletic accomplishments, and other factors) has not dropped in the post-9/11 years.

We need each of these programs to generate a quality force and prepare for future threats. In the words of former USMA Superintendent General Howard D. Graves, we must avoid the "mistake of trying to pit the . . . officer sources against one another as if they were quarter-backs competing for the starting position on the football team. To do so seriously misunderstands why we have four sources . . . [designed] to meet separate national needs, and make their own uniquely valuable contributions."[16] Officer manpower analysis experts are quick to advocate retention of all sources for another reason: unlike the corporate sector, which responds to market needs by acquiring personnel from a variety of sources, there is no lateral entry into the Army because the develop-mental structure and "industry-specific" training limit the ability of even a successful corporate leader to assimilate quickly into the culture.

A third fix that the military has implemented consists of financial and opportunity incentive programs for lieutenants and captains. For an exchange of three additional years of service, USMA and ROTC cadets receive the promise of graduate schooling, permanent change of station, or branch choice. Presently, 25 percent of ROTC and 15 percent of USMA cadets choose the graduate school option.[17] Besides improving continuance rates, this advanced civilian schooling will hopefully produce a better-educated, broader-thinking officer corps.

---

[16] Gen Howard Graves, USMA Superintendent from 1991–96, remarks on "Why West Point?" Available through USMA Public Affairs Office.

[17] Author telephone interview with the Deputy Director of OEMA, 15 September 2009.

For Army majors commissioned before 1998, however, there are fewer incentives available. In fact, according to a 2007 report by the GAO, the Navy and Air Force pay about ten times the amount the Army pays in retention-related incentives to equivalent ranks. As one Army major retorted in an *Armed Forces Journal* article, "A Navy lieutenant commander, the equivalent of an Army major, commissioned in 1997 could have received $121,000 in retention bonuses during his 12-year career; over that same time, an Army infantry officer would receive zero additional pay."[18] For those majors who have left active service, the Army is offering $10,000 bonus for a return to duty, but it has not offered incentives for those majors who have remained on active duty.

In summary, the quick fixes to officer retention—accelerating junior officer promotion, manipulating the officer supply channels, and incentive programs—only go so far in addressing the Chief of Staff of the Army's concerns. Exploring and addressing the root causes behind our manpower issues are a better long-term strategy for preserving the quality of our officer corps.

Root Causes of Understrength

Contrary to some popular discourse, the root causes of understrength status are not exclusively associated with the strain from operations in Iraq and Afghanistan. The downward trend started in the late 1990s and has precipitously fallen through to the present levels. This is due in great part to low continuation rates resulting from prosperous civilian opportunities, abundant nonmilitary funding and grants for college, and post–Cold War military downsizing in the "dot.com" 90s. In fact, Army majors debating on the Army Intermediate Level Education (Combined Arms College) blogs are quick to note that many factors influence their decisions to leave. While some confess that fulfilling civilian alternatives or the promise of higher compensation are motivation to leave, the following overarching themes are much more prevalent.

---

[18] Maj Myles Caggins, USA, "A Major Problem: Cent-sible Solutions for the Army's Major-Retention Dilemma," *Armed Forces Journal*, December 2008, http://www.armedforcesjournal.com/2008/12/ 3801581 (accessed 18 September 2009).

- Majors are usually at the age where they are starting or raising a family, and now more than ever, competing with their spouse for career prioritization and equal responsibility for domestic responsibilities. As mentioned above, repeat deployments have caused major strains in this regard.

- Many majors feel a communications gap between them and senior leaders. This problem might be remedied by improved mentoring. Because the battlefield is flatter and leadership is extraordinarily decentralized in the contemporary operating environment, communication between senior and intermediate leaders and their junior officers is mission essential. Genuine encouragement and empowerment of subordinates, according to many junior officers, are more important and yield higher return on investment than a pay incentive.

- A significant number of individuals feel their skills are under or poorly utilized, and this degrades the value of their undergraduate education as well as the niche skills and knowledge gained through civilian schooling or self-development. This stems in part from an anachronistic officer talent management framework in which we default to match "faces to spaces" and fail to associate talents and competencies with the needs of the Army.

- Our promotion system is frustrating to many officers. To rise in the ranks in the Army, one is required to pursue certain developmental job assignments. However, there are only 1,000 developmental O-4 jobs available, and about 15,000 majors competing for these slots. Without checking these blocks, the probability of promotion to O-6 and beyond is miniscule. While the Army officer rank structure is pyramidal in shape, this type of promotion system does not guarantee that the best and brightest rise to the highest ranks. Junior officers are cognizant of this shortfall and feel that the current system often penalizes individuals for trying to match their own skills and desires with the needs on the battlefield in the interest of national security objectives.

The convergence of the downsizing of our force two decades ago, the perceived and real social and psychological grievances (money, sex, job satisfaction, and support), the promising civilian alternatives, and the strains of combat is potentially leading us into a pending "major crisis," as one junior officer punned. Perhaps some of the complaints are typical of junior individuals, but if we consider General Casey and others' fears of a shallow, if not hollow, Army, all of these issues warrant further consideration.

Talent Management is the Key

One solution for improving the effectiveness of our soldiers in the short-term and the quality of our force in the long-term is to develop a comprehensive military personnel talent management system that goes beyond the faces-to-spaces approach. Talent management is a mindset that goes beyond rhetoric and toward a holistic and integrated approach to leveraging the greatest competitive advantage from people.[19] It will include special strategies to recruit, retain, and develop its pool of top talent. It is a key to leveraging a competitive advantage in peace and war.

The April 2009 SSI report put it this way:

> The U.S. Army's capacity to match officer talents to emerging challenges is antiquated. Its legacy personnel management tools were designed to align faces and spaces rather than talents and competency requirements. Today, the Army cannot fully employ talent it expends great resources to access, retain, and develop, nor does it articulate its talent requirements to officers so that they can structure their development in consonance with Army needs.[20]

In response to the call for improved talent management, a social networking Web 2.0 technology pilot program is underfoot in the Army Engineer branch. It attempts to allow officers to proactively list on an Internet profile page (similar to Facebook) their unique skill sets or hobbies that may be of use to the military. In contrast, Army officer records are limited to information such as source of commission and education data, awards, and training. Because of this limited available information for branch managers or commanders in the field, our organizational capacity to adapt or link the right person at the right place at the right time is impaired.

The 2009 SSI report advocating for this talent management program provides a useful example to illustrate the point of the Web 2.0 approach:

> The U.S. Army has been called upon to assume broad responsibility for reconstruction operations in Iraq, Afghanistan, and New Orleans. Efforts to adapt to these new missions have generated considerable demand for

---

[19] Kevin D. Stringer, "The War on Terror and the War for Officer Talent: Linked Challenges for the U.S. Army," The Land Warfare Papers, no. 67 (July 2008), http://www.ausa.org/Site Collection Documents/ILW%20Web-ExclusivePubs/Land%20Warfare%20Papers/LWP67.pdf (accessed 10 September 2009).

[20] Wardynski et al., "Officer Corps Strategy," 37.

officers who are professionally certified to guide structural, hydraulic, geological, transportation, power distribution, and other engineering projects. For example, while the Army carries hundreds of engineer officers on its ledgers, many of them lack the specific competencies required to conceive, plan, or execute reconstruction projects. Conversely, many engineer officers do possess these competencies, but as they stem from developmental experiences outside of those recorded within the current personnel information set, the Army does not "know" who or where they are in time of need.[21]

The talent management programs could help to improve efforts outside of the military ranks. Other services face this challenge as well. The same talent mismatch often exists in interagency task forces, command staffs, deployed units, and even among our multinational coalition efforts. Nor is the private sector immune to mismatching skills with organizational needs; talent management is a key "doctor's fix" for world-renowned management consulting firms such as McKinsey. Employing talent properly—whatever the service or organization—requires providing new challenges for promising officers, providing quality feedback and coaching, and weeding out poor performers. Right now, the Army is not fulfilling its mission in these regards. As the 2007 GAO report portends, "Without such a plan, the Army's ability to meet future mission requirements and achieve its transformation initiatives is uncertain."[22]

The Key

Military leaders wisely acknowledge the talent management— recruitment, training, retention, and employment—issues that we face today. There remain many existing challenges associated with the contemporary operating environment and overall force readiness, but the Army has proven its resiliency, and this era will hopefully be no different.

As illustrated, COIN and full-spectrum operations require that we invest great authority, responsibility, and resources at the lowest operational ranks. The challenge this presents to existing military hierarchical authority and management principles is exemplified at many levels: junior officers are

---

[21] Wardynski et al., "Officer Corps Strategy," 36.
[22] GAO, "Military Personnel," 7.

not fully trained to understand the totality of needs and responsibilities at their level, and their superiors are often inherently risk averse and unwilling or unused to delegating so much authority to the lowest levels. Fortunately, the troop-to-task oversight is changing. The experiences junior officers have gained in Iraq and Afghanistan and the Army's potential shift in talent management foretell a step in the right direction.

Additionally, militaries at war will invariably face personnel challenges, but history has shown that the U.S. armed forces have usually overcome manpower issues—albeit with a few growing pains along the way. Fortunately, Army leaders have taken many interim steps to preclude the onset of a hollow force, but our leaders can do more. First, better understanding of the evolving requirements and unique distribution of skills among junior officers serving on the frontline will help us to focus our recruitment efforts on individuals who are willing and capable of meeting our force needs. Second, understanding the root causes that lead to retention issues will help us to do a better job of preparing junior officers for the challenges, providing them with rank-appropriate rewards and incentives, and preventing the Army from losing the best of our corps to the private sector. Finally, a comprehensive talent management program will benefit both the officer corps and the Army. Putting the right person in the right place is tantamount to keeping the best and brightest on our team. As a recent study precisely concludes, "Talent management is a means to an end, not an end in itself. An officer strategy focused upon talent has but one purpose: to help the Army achieve its overall objectives."[23] Talent management—especially of the next generation of leaders—is the key.

---

[23] Col Casey Wardynski, Maj David S. Lyle, and LtCol Michael J. Colarusso (Ret), USA, "Talent: Implications For A U.S. Army Officer Corps Strategy" (Carlisle, PA: Strategic Studies Institute, November 2009), vi.

Chapter 9

Generalship and Counterinsurgency

by Thomas E. Ricks

When I was a teenager, I went to Afghanistan, where my father was teaching at Kabul University. He really enjoyed the Afghan people. I asked him one day, "What do you like so much about the Afghans?" And he said, "Oh, they're like the people I grew up with in rural Wyoming." These were the grandsons of pioneers. He knew a guy who had been brought in by the cattlemen to kill off the sheepmen and liked the valley so much that he stayed. "Basically," he said, "Afghans are Clint Eastwood with a turban."

By coincidence, I had the radio on when I was writing this, and a Leonard Cohen song came on: "Everybody Knows." It forced me to toss out what I was writing because I realized it was just a sermon on agility and adaptability, and everybody in this room knows that's what you need in a counterinsurgency (COIN)—creativity, flexibility, agility, and adaptability.

So the question I was thinking about more—the question that Leonard Cohen forced me to think about is this: What are the barriers for that? Why don't we have more of that? Why don't we have more of those people who can think self-critically, who can recognize situations in which the training and tools the military has given them are not adequate to the job and are able to find new and different tools?

I think especially at senior levels, this has been a problem. We've seen adaptive tactical and operational leaders. But what you also need is the leader who can recognize the absence of a decent strategy, which has plagued us both in Iraq and Afghanistan for several years. When you have a military that is tactically proficient without an adequate strategy to guide it, you effectively are riding at high speeds in a Ferrari without a steering wheel, and that's what we have been doing—that's what we did in Iraq for several years and what in many ways we are still doing in Afghanistan

I think in the current system we get adaptive senior leadership almost by mistake. You get a J. D. Alford, you get an H. R. McMaster surfacing. It's frequently ignored. If it is noticed, it's treated as a unique situation: "Oh, you can do that up in northwest Iraq, but you can't do that down here in Baghdad. It's a much different situation." I think there's no accident, by the way, that the first effective, sustained COIN campaigns in Iraq took place very far from Baghdad.

I also developed a COIN theory based on the old Johnny Cash song "A Boy Named Sue." If you really want an effective COIN leader, give him a first name like Julian or Herbert. Now, you may ask David—David Petraeus is not a weird name—but remember his high school nickname was Peaches—maybe that makes a good COIN leader.

So, what are the systemic barriers to this sort of adaptive, self-critical leadership? I think Paul Yingling offered some very good answers in his famous essay that ran in *Armed Forces Journal*. This is the book I'm currently working on, a history of American generalship from World War II to the present—the working title is *From George C. Marshall to Tommy R. Franks: What Up with That?*

The George C. Marshall model of generalship worked in World War II. It didn't look for agility, adaptability, or flexibility; it assumed it, because you are either successful, dead, or relieved within two months. But we no longer relieve people, so we've wound up with a general officer class, especially in the Army, that is full of Marshallesque, hard-charging, energetic conformists. They are well trained, but not necessarily well educated in the art of war.

I think the major reason for this is also Army-specific. The Army had this great training revolution in the 1980s when it regained tactical proficiency, especially with the training centers. But in the process of that, places like the National Training Center became the measure of an officer. I think the Army, to a surprising degree, confused battalion command with generalship. So you have people like Tommy Franks, being the best example, who really thought that strategy was a job that someone on staff did for you. I would see that as akin to having a general who thinks that somebody else should issue orders for him.

Clausewitz tells us that the supreme and sole task of the senior leader is to understand the nature of the conflict in which he or she is engaged and adjust to it. Tommy Franks did not. Tommy Franks thought that taking the enemy capital was how you won a war. This is a little bit like Major General George B. McClellan going after Richmond in the Civil War. Franks thought that taking Kabul and pushing al-Qaeda into Pakistan was a strategic victory. Why anybody thought that pushing al-Qaeda from Afghanistan into a bigger country that had nuclear weapons was a good idea is beyond me.

Then, he goes to Iraq and does the same thing. Let's go to Baghdad and then spike the ball at the fifty-yard line. I think Franks went zero for two. And the question is this: why that guy rose to four stars and was allowed to lead two wars? I would say a system that produces a Tommy Franks is not a system that is producing adaptive, agile, and creative leaders. So how do you change the system?

First, I think you restore accountability. The Marines have less of a problem with this than the Army does, I think, because the Marines come out of a maritime tradition, and if there's one thing the Navy is good at, it is relieving skippers who ground their ships. You need accountability. You need to know what success looks like. You need to know what failure looks like.

In Iraq, for several years, and in Afghanistan perhaps still, we did not know what a successful tour of duty really looked like. For several years, there seemed to be no relationship between performance in Iraq and subsequent promotions. In fact, going back to the discussion of risk aversion, the commander in Iraq who played it careful during a one-year tour probably fared better in promotions than the risk-taker, which is not what you want in wartime. You don't want recklessness, but you want calculated risk taking. You certainly do not want a commander who keeps his head down, plays for a tie, and tries to get out of Dodge with that Bronze Star and a successful tour-of-duty report.

Back in 2005, Kalev "Gunner" Sepp and Colonel, now Brigadier General-to-be, Bill Hix did a study of battalion, brigade, and regimental commanders in Iraq and how successful they were in implementing COIN doctrine. The conclusion of the Sepp-Hix report was that one-third of commanders got it, one-third were trying to get it but weren't really, and one-third didn't get it and didn't want to get it. That means in late 2005, two-thirds of our force in Iraq was ineffective and perhaps counterproductive.

So, I think for accountability, relief is a neglected tool. I think actually even Petraeus and General Raymond T. Odierno in command in Iraq shied away from this. I was told that when a unit was ineffective in COIN, they'd find something else for it to do rather than make it more effective, especially if it only had a couple of months left in the tour. It was just too late, it took too much energy, let's just move them over to the corner and do something else with them.

Relief used to be very common in the U.S. Army. During World War II, seventeen division commanders and at least four corps commanders were relieved. But relief also did not carry the weight it does today. You could relieve an officer without killing his career.

For example, Major General Terry de la Mesa Allen, commander of the Big Red One—the 1st Infantry Division—in central Sicily during the summer of 1943 won the first battle that American forces fought against Germans on European soil. For his efforts, at the end of the battle, he and his assistant division commander, Teddy Roosevelt Jr., were relieved. Yet a year later, Terry de la Mesa Allen was commanding another division—the 104th—across northern France, and he did a very good job. Another assistant division commander, Brigadier General Sam Williams, was not only relieved but was demoted, stayed in the Army, and retired later as a three star.

So I think relief can be seen differently as a management tool, not just as basically putting a gun to a guy's head and killing his career. I don't think you do anyone a favor, especially that person's subordinates, by keeping him in a job he shouldn't have.

The final systemic change, I think, you need in COIN leadership is unity of command. This is edict one according to French military officer and scholar David Galula. We have never had unity of command in Iraq or Afghanistan. I would like to see a proconsul. I would like to see somebody in charge of the national effort, not only because Galula says you should have somebody in charge of the national effort, but also because he says it is essential to have a civilian in charge of the national effort as, ultimately, all questions are going to be political and have to be judged and measured in political terms.

We've had civilian authority and military authority in Iraq frequently at odds. This is not just a problem of civilians. I actually think that L. Paul Bremer tried to carry out the national command authority's wishes to revolutionize Iraq and to transform it into a beacon of democracy that would transform the Middle East. The U.S. military rightly assessed that mission to be insane, and so the military shirked the duty of carrying it out and said, "No, we do stability." This has often put the military authority and the civilian authority in disagreement. You can paper this over with handshakes, or you can really have people resolve to work together as Petraeus and Crocker did, but I think until you have a real unity of effort at the top, you're always going to be having a jerry-rigged effort.

Part V
Counterinsurgency Leadership in Afghanistan

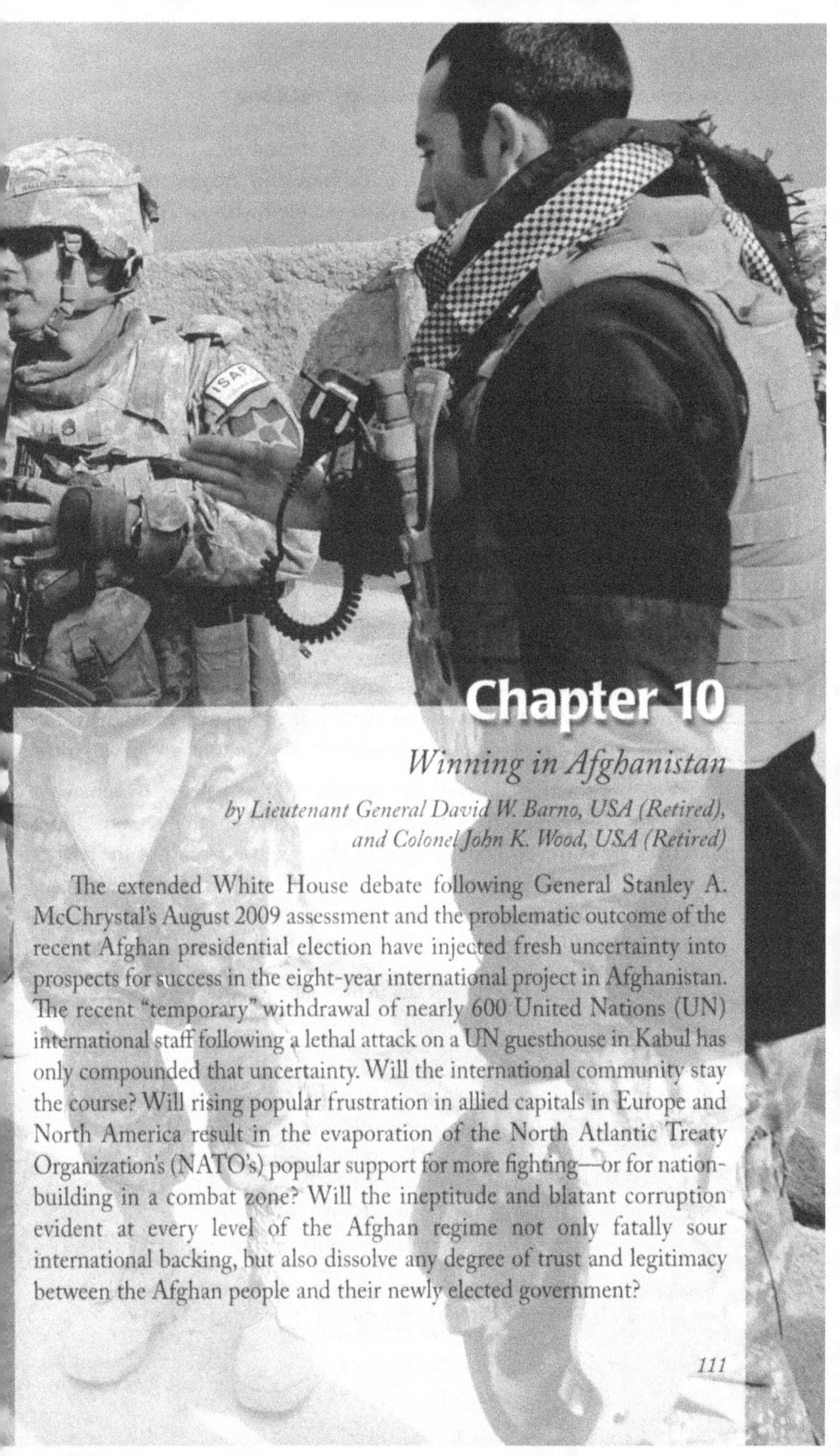

Chapter 10

Winning in Afghanistan

by Lieutenant General David W. Barno, USA (Retired),
and Colonel John K. Wood, USA (Retired)

The extended White House debate following General Stanley A. McChrystal's August 2009 assessment and the problematic outcome of the recent Afghan presidential election have injected fresh uncertainty into prospects for success in the eight-year international project in Afghanistan. The recent "temporary" withdrawal of nearly 600 United Nations (UN) international staff following a lethal attack on a UN guesthouse in Kabul has only compounded that uncertainty. Will the international community stay the course? Will rising popular frustration in allied capitals in Europe and North America result in the evaporation of the North Atlantic Treaty Organization's (NATO's) popular support for more fighting—or for nation-building in a combat zone? Will the ineptitude and blatant corruption evident at every level of the Afghan regime not only fatally sour international backing, but also dissolve any degree of trust and legitimacy between the Afghan people and their newly elected government?

Rising skepticism concerning American and allied intentions have helped fuel the resurgence of the Taliban and created political and military space for its expansion. When coupled with an Afghan's long-standing intolerance of foreign troops, our recent history of abandonment—whether real or perceived—accelerates the Afghans' impatience and makes our diplomatic, political, and military efforts much more challenging. Regardless of the tactics chosen to pursue the American objectives in Afghanistan and the region, clearly establishing through words and deeds that the United States is and will be a reliable long-term partner is essential and should form the basis of any strategy. Countering the Taliban, assisting the Afghans' efforts to restore legitimacy to their government, developing and maintaining civilian and military unity of effort, and reframing the public narrative on Afghanistan can only be built upon the Afghan's trust in the willingness of the United States to remain engaged for the long term.

Defining Core Goals

Any discussion of reversing the downward trajectory in Afghanistan must start with a discussion of objectives. What is "winning"? Can we "win"?

Winning for the United States in this context equates to achieving American policy objectives in Afghanistan and in the region. Those objectives are currently under review in Washington as part of the overall reappraisal of the U.S. effort following the McChrystal assessment. In his landmark 27 March speech outlining U.S. goals at the outset of his presidency, President Barack H. Obama depicted those goals as follows:

> And if the Afghan government falls to the Taliban—or allows al-Qaeda to go unchallenged—that country will again be a base for terrorists who want to kill as many of our people as they possibly can.... For the Afghan people, a return to Taliban rule would condemn their country to brutal governance, international isolation, a paralyzed economy, and the denial of basic human rights to the Afghan people—especially women and girls. The return in force of al-Qaeda terrorists who would accompany the core Taliban leadership would cast Afghanistan under the shadow of perpetual violence.[1]

---

[1] Barack H. Obama, "Remarks by the President on a New Strategy for Afghanistan and Pakistan" (speech, Dwight D. Eisenhower Executive Office Building, Washington, DC, 27 March 2009).

His white paper accompanying the speech outlined a core goal of disrupting, dismantling, and defeating al-Qaeda and its safe havens in Pakistan, and preventing their return to Pakistan or Afghanistan.

Our characterization of the strategic goals for the United States argues for a broader regional perspective and comprises the following points:

- The Taliban and al-Qaeda defeated in the region and denied usable sanctuary, and further attacks on the United States or allies precluded;

- Pakistan stabilized as a long-term partner that is economically viable, friendly to the United States, no longer an active base for international terrorism, and in control of its nuclear weapons;

- The NATO alliance preserved with its role in Afghanistan recast into a politically sustainable set of objectives;

- The Afghan government stabilized as a legitimate state in the eyes of the Afghan people, capable of exercising effective governance and control of its territory;

- Regional states confident of U.S. staying power and commitment as their partner in the multifaceted regional struggle against violent extremism; and

- The United States' regional circle of friends expanded, and the influence of enemies (e.g., violent extremists) diminished.

These goals are derived from a long-term perspective of U.S. strategic interests in the region, and are oriented toward a positive set of objectives leading in the direction of long-term regional stability. The potential threat emanating from regional instability in a part of the world where two heavily armed nuclear powers are locked in a perpetual cold war should drive us toward a goal more broadly focused than simply quashing al-Qaeda. The remainder of this paper, however, focuses on the immediate challenge before us in Afghanistan.

The Situation in Afghanistan

Four main factors define the current situation. First and foremost is the persistent, resilient, and adaptive insurgency that capitalizes on the fear and uncertainty about the future of the Afghan people. This insurgency is strengthened by the weakness and corruption of the Afghan government, and it strives to outlast the diverse international efforts arrayed against it: "The Americans have all the wristwatches, but the Taliban have all the time." Second, a growing crisis of confidence among the Afghan people is fed by a lack of trust in their government and persistent fears of abandonment by the United States and the international community. The third factor is a continued lack of unity of effort by international military and civilian efforts. Integration of efforts is largely nonexistent, and even coordination has been strikingly limited. Lack of results on the ground reinforces this harsh judgment. Finally, the vision for success in Afghanistan—the endgame—is unclear to both the international and Afghan publics. Lack of clearly defined aims creates confusion among Americans, our allies, and the Afghan people, and bolsters the Taliban's confidence that the insurgency can and will prevail. Put simply, if we succeed—what will the next day look like? Have we aligned our leadership, resources, and strategy to deliver the best outcome? In sum, these four factors threaten to jeopardize our entire enterprise in Afghanistan. The battle for Afghanistan is winnable, but will demand all of the resolve that both the Afghan people and the international community can muster in order to succeed.

Four Major Challenges

1. Defeat the Taliban Strategy

Put simply, the Taliban leadership's strategy is to "run out the clock" on international involvement in Afghanistan. The leaders of the Taliban are convinced that they are winning, that they have the initiative, and that they can succeed by being the "last man standing" in Afghanistan on the day after all outsiders depart. History is on their side. Policy debates at home which question our purpose and resolve in Afghanistan—and which constantly talk about exit options—reinforce the Taliban's confidence in the correctness of their strategy. We must defeat this strategy by declaring an end state that centers on a long-term U.S. and international presence focused on assuring regional stability—using diplomatic, economic, and military tools (robust security assistance combined with limited kinetic operations).

As stated succinctly in the recent U.S. counterinsurgency (COIN) manual, "Tactical success guarantees nothing."[2] Defeating the Taliban strategy requires more than simple attrition warfare or remote-controlled missile strikes. While the Taliban wants to sap the will of the international community, increasing violence against the International Security Assistance Force (ISAF) and the Afghan forces is also intended to increase the level of intimidation and uncertainty among the Afghan population. A population-centric COIN strategy recognizes the Taliban's intent, and strives to separate the insurgents from the population and increase the human security dimension—personal security, health and education, access to resources, governance, and economic opportunity. A population-centric approach aims to transform the environment and deny the Taliban the opportunity to erode the population's sense of well-being in the societal, governmental, and economic spheres of national activity. This requires significant nonmilitary resources, persistence, and patience. Success also requires a strong and lasting demonstration of resolve in the face of casualties and other significant setbacks.

ISAF should prioritize the allocation of military forces to counter the Taliban's strategic targeting of Kandahar City, Khowst Province, and other population and transportation centers. Focusing deployments of ISAF and the Afghan National Army to key population centers—including key areas in the north and west—while accepting tactical risks in less populated or geographically isolated areas, will help restore security among the people and work toward closing the trust deficit. The prioritization must be done in close coordination with United Nations Assistance Mission in Afghanistan (UNAMA), the Government of the Islamic Republic of Afghanistan, and the aid community. Military power alone, regardless of the size of the force deployed, will not defeat the Taliban. Only a well-coordinated and well-targeted campaign of expanded security, governance, rule of law, and economic opportunity built around controlling the major population centers and restoring hope and optimism among the people will succeed in defeating the Taliban. Success requires that the Afghan people have confidence in their personal security, health and education, access to resources, governance, and economic future—a broad human security portfolio. The Afghan people, down to the local level, are the ultimate arbiters of success in Afghanistan.

---

[2] U.S. Army and U.S. Marine Corps, *Counterinsurgency*, Army Field Manual 3-24/Marine Corps Warfighting Publication 3-33.5 (Washington, DC: Department of the Army and Marine Corps Combat Development Command, 2006), 1-28.

Convincing these ultimate arbiters—the Afghan people—and defeating the Taliban's strategy requires an effective communications strategy. The difficulty of persuading local populations and communicating effective messages of strength and resolve in a foreign culture cannot be overstated. An effective communications strategy can only be delivered by Afghans themselves—and must be underwritten by coalition deeds and acceptable behavior, not just hollow rhetoric. Actions inevitably speak louder than talking points. The most powerful message is the conduct of the various actors on the ground: U.S., Afghan, and Coalition security forces; the Afghan government; and the various governmental and nongovernmental development and reconstruction agencies. As the perceived legitimacy of the Afghan government has diminished, successful execution of an Afghan-led communications campaign has become increasingly difficult. It is therefore equally important that we assist the next Afghan government in efforts to rebuild the trust and confidence of the Afghan people toward their own institutions.

2. Assist the Next Afghan Government to Rebuild Trust and Confidence with the Afghan People

The people of Afghanistan have lost much of their trust and confidence in the current Afghan government. We must focus our diplomatic and assistance efforts in Kabul on reforming the "next" government to better meet the people's expectations, with special emphasis on anticorruption measures. In local areas across Afghanistan— in the provinces and districts—we must work hand-in-hand with local Afghan government structures to build capacity and to help them deliver results that people can feel. If the international community is seen by the Afghan people to be blithely supporting a new government that is every bit as corrupt as the current one, our efforts will lack legitimacy there and at home. Internally, reestablishing the legitimacy of the government helps repair the trust deficit opened over the last several years of accelerating corruption. Externally, a credible central government is essential to maintaining the commitment of western allies and partners. Reestablishing popular trust and confidence in the central government, although remote from many Afghans, will provide a powerful counterstroke to the insurgency.

The recurrent debate between strengthening the central government versus strengthening capacity at the local level must be ended. Afghanistan requires a capable national government in Kabul and workable, legitimate local institutions at the provincial, district, and village levels. Models for such a structure exist in Afghan history over the centuries, most recently in the 1960s and early 1970s. Action in this realm must be two-pronged: Kabul and the central government serving as the top-down focus of the Kabul-based international community; and provincial and district-levels serving as the bottom-up focus, enabled (and primarily led) by military efforts.

Military civil affairs units joined by a select number of appropriately trained and equipped civilian volunteers, with adequate legal authorities, should focus on improving the accountability and performance of Afghan provincial and district governance, catalyzing economic development, and improving the rule of law. Civilian volunteers will often be at the same levels of risk as the military units with whom they are partnered—which reinforces the need for military-led efforts during "in-conflict" (rather than "postconflict") reconstruction and development capabilities.

While embedded with the Afghan-led communications campaign, this new approach should be directly connected to the Afghan National Development Strategy goals with Coalition military forces providing an essential behind-the-scenes role: leadership from the rear. Only by integrating all of these civil-military efforts in one team will synergy and effectiveness be achieved. The Coalition military commander must be partnered with his Afghan National Army counterpart and the local Afghan governmental leader—be it provincial governor or district administrator. The disjointed approaches employed to date—dividing military and civil (and even Afghan) enterprises in the face of a resurgent enemy—have taken us to the brink of failure. It is past time to make the bold shift required to ensure success.

3. Establish Military and Civilian Unity of Effort

This is most important at the local level. If effective, it reinforces the restoration of trust between government and people. General McChrystal's eventual plan can create this local unity of effort for the first time by fusing all players into a whole of collective ownership at the district and provincial levels. Although in many respects this may initially infringe upon Afghan prerogatives, it will be judged by local populations by its benefits to them. This effort is an imperative to turn perceptions around at the grassroots level.

The August 2009 approval by NATO of an operational three-star headquarters is a significant recognition of what has been a persistent military shortfall over the past three years: a lack of operational unity of effort in the theater. Further coordination with the UNAMA and nongovernmental organizations is necessary to synchronize and deliver a fully coordinated civilian-military COIN campaign.

A more unified military and civilian effort also assists the communications effort. Clear chains of command and authority, commonly agreed goals and objectives, and aggressive but coordinated execution reinforce communication of key messages, give the Afghan government a well-defined set of partners, and indicate to the population unwavering seriousness of purpose. Unity of effort may further accelerate delivery of essential services to the population and counteract claims of inefficiency and corruption within the donor community.

4. Reframe the Public Narrative on Afghanistan

What is the endgame for the United States in the region? Until we can clearly answer this question, for ourselves and for our friends in the region, we have no sound policy. We do not have a clear definition of success, and worse we have signaled that "exit" is the ultimate goal. This is strategically unsound and undercuts virtually any strategy we pursue.

The rationale for staying and winning in Afghanistan has become muddled in the United States and among our allies abroad. National leaders must clearly articulate our endgame (presence, not exit) and lay out for our peoples the serious risks attendant to failure. Several seemingly attractive options are now on the table; the costs of failure attached to each are enormous, yet are rarely articulated. The moral imperative of not abandoning the Afghan people, especially the women, to the depredations of the Taliban once more must be part of this debate. The risks of a regional, proxy civil war and a deadly spread of instability into Pakistan must be clearly stated. Finally, the risk of loss of credibility to the United States and the international community would have repercussions far beyond the borders of Afghanistan and South Asia, and would influence every major foreign policy issue for years to come.

The fundamental flaw in any U.S. approach to Afghanistan or Pakistan remains the lack of confidence in American staying power, demonstrated by the common question from Afghans of every stripe: "You Americans are not going to abandon us again, are you?" This fundamental uncertainty drives the Pakistanis (and now perhaps, Afghans) to weigh all national security decisions in terms of the question: "What will this look like the day after the Americans leave?" (This is a repeated phrase.) We must directly confront these fears by unequivocally asserting our intended long-term presence and posture. Signaling that our long-term goal is "exit" deeply undercuts our influence on all actors and bolsters the Taliban's strategy. We must craft a clear picture of what success looks like for our friends across the region that includes persistence and commitment.

Now is the Time

Success or failure in Afghanistan will set the terms of further U.S. involvement in the region for a generation. Will American credibility suffer a fatal blow among our regional friends? Are they strong enough to stand alone in the face of a resurgent extremist movement spanning the region? Will the NATO alliance survive a defeat and withdrawal from Afghanistan? Will our extremist adversaries be catalyzed, both in the region and globally, by their success in ejecting westerners from this part of the world? Does this victory over the West energize a rebirth of violent Islamic extremism where many see it waning today?

Short-term gains in avoiding the immediate cost in blood and treasure in Afghanistan may well result in longer term and more dangerous threats produced by our departure. There are no cheap and easy solutions. There are immense costs associated with withdrawal before we achieve our objectives. The risks of any alternatives to the COIN approach outlined by General McChrystal must be clearly and forcefully debated and understood. These risks affect not only our role in the region among friends and adversaries, they also affect our oldest alliances and the credibility of our relationships around the globe.

Losing in Afghanistan after more than eight years of major international effort will create potentially horrific results: an insecure Pakistan, a return to deep sanctuary for al-Qaeda, increased regional instability across south and central Asia, a lack of confidence in American staying power and military prowess, and a fragmentation of NATO and the transatlantic alliance. Failure is truly not an option.

Now is the time to reverse the trends of the past several years, to refocus our national resolve, and to regain the trust of the Afghan people so that they and their government can repulse the rising influence of the Taliban and restore the chance for victory in this crucial region of the world. Winning is possible—but we are facing our last opportunity to do so.

Chapter 11

Advising Afghan Military Forces

by Colonel Jeffery M. Haynes, USMC

My remarks are based on my experience in 2008 as the 201st Corps, Afghan National Army (ANA) senior advisor. As senior advisor, I advised the corps commander and I had a staff that advised his staff. I also had about 600 to 700 advisors from six different countries sprinkled throughout Regional Command (RC) East and RC Capital. That is what you know it as. I know it as 201st Corps Area of Operations (AO). That is part of our problem; we view this as a U.S. problem, not an Afghan problem.

This chapter will take us all the way down to the tactical level, maybe even lower if you can get lower than that. But what I want to do is compel decision makers to take action right away to give the ANA more of this fight. I think that is one of our fundamental flaws. It is based partly on the personality of American servicemembers because we want to do it ourselves when we go somewhere. That is what attracted us to the Army and the Marine Corps. Well, in some cases, we have taken that too far and we are not giving the ANA an opportunity to make a difference.

We need to give them more ownership of the fight or, in some cases, insist they take more ownership of it. We are not getting an adequate return on our investment with the ANA. We have spent billions of dollars. There are pockets of brilliance. But there are areas where they need huge improvement.

That lack of effectiveness is based, in my mind, on the following four reasons. And again, this is 2008 in the AO in which I was operating.

- There is a lack of ANA leadership, accountability, and initiative—and integrity, in some cases.

- I think we are using the wrong metric by using capability milestones. These do not measure the ANA's combat effectiveness.

- We have extreme variations in advisor competence. We are not always putting the right people over there with the right training. When we do, it is a machine and it works well. When we don't, it doesn't work as well.

- The theme throughout is the ANA does not have a sense of ownership of the problem.

Afghan National Army Leadership

Command selection in the ANA, at least when I left, was partially based on ethnicity. There are probably some good reasons for that based on their history. That is in policy. In practice, it is based a lot on who you know. As a result, it is difficult for a senior commander to hold his subordinate commanders accountable because they can easily do an end-around to someone at the Ministry of Defense and General Staff and undo the corrections the corps or brigade commander has tried to make.

Officer accountability is extremely uneven. We need to help them get that right. There is a lot of cronyism, a lot of "who do you know and who are you connected to"—not in all cases, but in too many cases.

This inability to fairly reward or punish breeds a lack of trust between the leader and the led. That inhibits operational effectiveness and initiative. It also affects distribution of fuel, supplies, tactical orders, promotions, command selection, and so on.

The Metric

More important, we need to talk about improving ANA effectiveness in combat. Unfortunately, we measure this by ratings that are geared for force generation. They are called *capability milestone ratings*. It is how many people they have, how many trucks, how many weapons, their logistics capability, their training capability, and a little bit of subjectivity in there about leadership. But this is a U.S.-centric tool for force generation, which is good when you are allocating resources. It is not good when you are measuring ANA performance.

It is not good because the ANA commanders are mildly interested in capability milestone ratings. As advisors, it makes us crazy. We do the monthly math drill. It gets sent up to higher authorities. Supposedly, the president hears about it. That is what they used to threaten us with. But, you know, it didn't make a difference because my Afghan counterpart only knew about it when I went up and told him about it. In some cases, they don't want to be one of the highest milestones ratings because they are scared we are going to leave and take all the money.

Despite all these challenges, though, there are some pockets of brilliance within the ANA. Of the three brigades in 201st Corps, consider one of them, General Zameri's 3d Brigade. A very good commander, he operates primarily in the Sarobi area. Uzbin is extreme eastern Kabul Province, about sixty miles east of Kabul. That is where the French got in that bad fight in August 2008. He operates out there. He also operates in the Tagab Valley of Kapisa Province just north of there, a very critical area.

With a very strong dose of what journalist Andrew Lubin calls "muscular mentoring," 3d Brigade developed, conceived, executed, and continues to execute a very holistic, integrated counterinsurgency (COIN) campaign in the Tagab Valley.

In the first phase, Zameri led this campaign with security and development, which I thought was fascinating. It wasn't clear-hold-build. You start talking clear-hold-build to a pretty savvy Afghan COIN operator, and he just thinks you are another linear-minded Westerner. In fact, I agreed with his approach once I saw it in action. He uses that development to co-opt the population, bring them to him, and provide intelligence at the same time he is securing. Clear is the wrong tactical task anyway. I see plenty of

Marines in here. We know what *clear* means. Clear is the wrong tactical task in a COIN. That means we are killing and breaking everything.

Fortunately, Zameri was beyond that type of thinking. But the components of his campaign included expeditionary camps. We borrowed some HESCO barriers from other units who weren't looking. I gave them to the Afghans. The Afghans went out and started building their own forward operating bases (FOBs). It worked very well. It signals that permanent presence to the population, that the ANA is there to stay. They also built observation posts (OPs). Being from Texas, we love to fly our flag. Well, the boys in Afghanistan, they get on that OP and they fly the flag, and the locals see the Afghan flag on the high ground and it gives them a sense of permanence and security. The locals love to see the Afghan army up there. They don't like seeing the police. I wasn't a police mentor. I won't talk much about it. But I will tell you they like the army in their battlespace.

The campaign also included patrol and security operations that disrupted an enemy primarily from the north and east. They operated often with the French battalion up there. They worked very well. The Afghans also did road improvements, which facilitated the movement of security forces that was absolutely critical and also facilitated goods to market. Part of the campaign involves increasing business.

The campaign, again, a great example of integrated Afghan leadership, included local farmer training by nongovernmental organizations (NGOs). Our NGOs came in and, partly facilitated by the embedded training teams (ETTs), taught the locals how to increase their crop yield with the pomegranates there. They also integrated or introduced saffron as a replacement for poppy.

All of this was supported by some very savvy Afghan 3d Brigade officers using the media. They got on the radio and spoke to the people in their language. What I loved about that is that it drew General Zameri to the population. But the 101st Airborne Division (the Combined Joint Task Force in command of U.S. forces in Afghanistan in 2008) wanted me to send them the message so they could approve it. That didn't go over well. An Afghan is not going to have the United States approve a message in his own language to his own people over a civilian radio station. The campaign was also supported by town hall meetings, *shuras*[1] maybe, talks by the Corps religious officer, medical civic action programs, and humanitarian assistance deliveries. The bottom line—it was integrated.

The population in Tagab now believes in the Afghan government through the ANA, and the population is helping the army deny the insurgents. Soon after this campaign started, we began receiving cell phone calls. General Zameri received calls from locals telling us where improvised explosive devices (IEDs) were planted. The IEDs were actually there and were found and reduced by ANA engineers.

The campaign tells us that with good ANA leadership and good creative mentorship, all those traits we have talked about that COIN leaders and advisors have to have, that the ANA can transform a valley once beholden to the enemy to where their lives are improving, an area where the population is proud of the ANA. We also integrated some air assault operations in Afghan helicopters with Afghan pilots, mentored, but nobody behind the stick.

Now, let's compare General Zameri's Tagab campaign to what was going on in Nangarhar and Nuristan Provinces about the same time. In the spring of 2008, we had terrible Afghan leadership in place. I won't give you all the details. Again, I had to relieve an advisor from another service and put Lieutenant Colonel Anthony Terlizzi out there to help fix this. Bottom line, we had criminal activity—blatant criminal activity, total disregard for the mission. It was putting my people at risk.

I was working with the corps commander to try to get some of these guys relieved. Of course, it was an Afghan decision. I was trying to influence that. He was having a heck of a time—back to that connection, that cronyism. We had particular ethnic groups that were well connected. We couldn't get rid of them. After multiple trips to the general staff, I had to personally tell senior leaders on the ANA staff in Kabul either the *kandak*[2] commander starts leading or I am pulling the ETT. That sent absolute shockwaves that I was going to pull an ETT and leave the kandak in Nuristan. When you pull the ETT, you pull out access to enablers. You pull out cash. Sometimes you pull out the ability to buy food and fuel for the ANA.

---

[1] *Shura* means "consultation" in Arabic; in general usage, it denotes a consultative council or assembly.
[2] A *kandak* is the Afghan equivalent of a battalion.

My point is that it takes savvy, strong-willed leaders who can stand up and do the right thing. And I use myself as an example. But below me, there are many, many more great things. There are great things going on by my people who put their lives at risk every single day.

The Advisors

We cannot shortchange the advising effort at all. It has to take a priority. It has to take a priority in manning and training. Our advisors need to model professionalism in everything they do. I commanded twenty-three teams from six different countries. It is amazing the different levels of experience we have out there. And you can't really build a model based on partnering or not partnering or advising because our advisors are so varied. We have got to fix this.

Advisors have got to leave their egos at the door. They have got to be more interested in ANA success than their own success. They have to view their success by their Afghan counterparts' success. They have to understand Afghan culture. They have to understand ANA culture. The two are slightly different. They have to be creative. They have to have perseverance. They have to be able to endure.

They have to be able to engage the Coalition. This may be upsetting to some people, but sometimes the Coalition is a problem for the Afghan army. Sometimes they belittle them. Sometimes they want to put them in the corner. Sometimes they want to misuse them or relegate them to the back. We can't have that.

Ownership

As we grow the ANA, I recommend we make our units larger in Afghanistan because we don't have enough adequate leadership to go around. Eventually, we have to grow more kandaks, but for the time being, let's take a 649-man battalion, let's make it 900. We just don't have enough leaders to go around. Plus, there is a little history of defection with Afghan units.

Number two, give the ANA battlespace today. Right now, give them battlespace within capability. Have a competent adjacent unit with them. You had better have good advisors to give the ANA battlespace now. I think they already have battlespace in Tagab, but giving them battlespace will trigger that initiative, and an ANA commander will not want to lose face if he owns the problem.

Number three, we have got to drop the term *battlespace owner*. It is offensive. It is wrong. I don't think it is tactical in any dictionary I have ever read for terms and graphics. But the U.S. battlespace owner doesn't own the battlespace. If he did, we wouldn't have so many doggone bad guys in it. But it sends the message to the Afghans that this is a Coalition problem. Once we got it figured out and I explained to the Afghans what that really means— they manage the forward air controllers and they help us out with fires, which is certainly important, and casualty evacuation all too often for my ETTs. That is extremely important. But we change the name every time. Bayonet becomes Duke. Warrior changes to Cyclone. My favorite, Gladiator went to Gladius. Try doing that through an interpreter to your Afghan counterpart.

Number four, beware of overpartnering. I believe partnering should be done early in the life cycle, but there is no substitute for aggressive, motivated, confident, stubborn ETTs hand-in-hand with their Afghans every day. This partnering business, I think it sounds good, but too much of it is based on the personality of the partner unit's commander. And some are going to be really good. Some are just going to want them to guard the FOB.

The ANA see us as very rich and we are, having all the toys. They will be glad to sit on the FOB because they are there for a lifetime. We are there for a year. Every new Coalition unit comes in with their vision of how they are going to save the world. They are all about letting you have it. So if you overpartner, I caution you to just be careful.

Number five, metrics. Our metric does not need to be capability milestone ratings. It's pretty simple. It needs to be how much battlespace the ANA controls.

Number six, we need to have brigade- and corps-level mentors who can mentor Tagab-like campaigns. You need to pick the right valleys. This is a valley fight. You need to help the ANA through some human terrain analysis. Understanding the culture, marry that with the innate understanding of the Afghans and their understanding of the culture. Pick the right valleys and endeavor to transform them. The people in Afghanistan like the ANA. They like helicopters. They like that OP behind me. They like to see that. They don't care if it doesn't look good and it is not per the 6-4 or Military Decision Making Process-1. If it is a clunky, ugly Afghan solution, that is much better than a perfect Coalition solution.

While these campaigns are going on, the mentors should be out acquiring other enablers—NGOs, U.S. Provincial Reconstruction Teams (PRTs)—working with the Coalition to get that unity of effort to help the Afghans implement a holistic COIN program and campaign.

And last, I have alluded to it already, we need to give the ANA enablers. I tried to start an ANA PRT. The ANA need their own PRT. If they are going to take the COIN fight, they need to do COIN-like things. Now, it needs to be heavily mentored, of course. We need to give the ANA funds for projects, again, heavily mentored. I am not that naïve. But we need them to have what I call COIN enablers so they can further implement more Tagabs.

At the end of the day, this is what I think we need: strong ANA leaders, obviously, encouraged and mentored by strong advisors to take the ANA to the next level. We need advisors who understand the larger picture, understand the long-term picture that it is about ANA development, about giving the ANA within capacity—not ahead of their time, but within capacity—ownership of the fight. If we don't do this, we are going to be there for a very long time. Our grandkids are going to be there.

Part VI
The 2009 Afghan Presidential Election

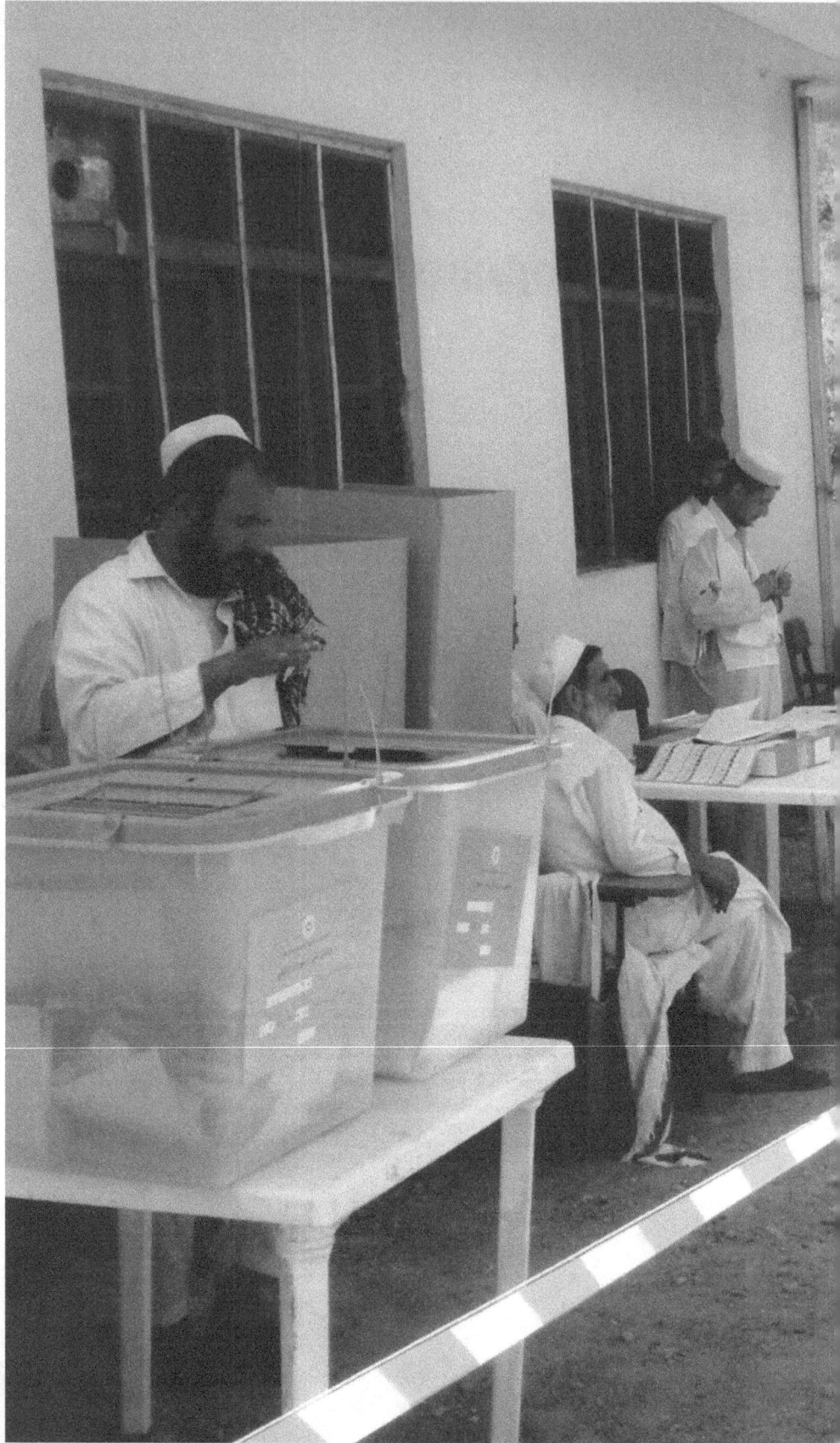

Chapter 12

The Afghan Election and the Future of Afghanistan's Leadership: A Discussion

Robert D. Kaplan, Clare Lockhart, Amin Tarzi, and Jeffrey Gedmin

Robert D. Kaplan

When we organized this panel some months ago, we assumed that the Afghan elections would be in hindsight by now, and that we would move on to the next story, so to speak, with finality.

That has not happened. Without putting too fine a point on it, the Afghan elections, rather than further legitimizing the Afghan government and power structure, have thrown its legitimacy into doubt. And I am being very polite on that score. Yet, at the same time, one of the fundamental points of realist theory going all the way back to Thucydides is that you work with the material at hand. Not only can you only work with the material at hand, you have to work with the material at hand at that specific moment.

Had we made different decisions six or nine months ago, we would have had, perhaps, more alternatives in terms of Afghan leadership than we have now. But let me tell you a bit about Afghanistan's past. There is a cliché out there that Afghanistan was always a barbaric place. It was never really a country. It is about building something from nothing.

Three-and-a-half decades ago, I traveled through Afghanistan as a visitor, and I was able to go all over the country by bus in complete safety on major and minor roads. This was a time when malaria eradication was almost complete, when Afghanistan had a fairly stable government under a monarch who controlled the major roads, major towns, and about 50 to 75 percent of the territory around there.

There were several decades of the twentieth century where Afghanistan was a viable state just as there were several decades in the same era when Iraq was close to being a viable democracy. The Afghans yearned for this pre-mid-1970s order so much that in 1996, when the Taliban came in, they initially embraced them thinking that they would bring order to the country. Well, they did, but it was more or less the order of the grave.

There are real themes in Afghan history that argue that all is not lost, that something can be done. Let me note that many of these questions about elections and government legitimacy go back to a 1968 Yale University Press book by Professor Samuel Huntington, *Political Order in Changing Societies*. Huntington wrote that to hold elections is not necessarily progressive. Progressive is the building of institutions. And how do you build institutions? Institutions often come through authoritarian regimes that become less authoritarian as time goes on. One has examples in Taiwan, South Korea, Chile, and other places. So these philosophical questions that Huntington posed over four decades ago are still with us.

Clare Lockhart

I absolutely agree with Robert Kaplan that we need to step back from the question of elections as an event and look at the question of institutions that allow participation, empowerment, and governance in general.

Over the last weeks, we have seen something of a false debate about whether we are trying to create a Valhalla or a Switzerland on the one hand, or whether we should leave the country to anarchy and chaos on the other. I think the question is neither of those things. It is the question of what is appropriate governance for the context.

If we look back over the recent years, over the last decades, and over the centuries in Afghanistan, we do see that governance of high or reasonable standard is absolutely possible. As we just heard, anyone who has spent time in the villages in Afghanistan understands the enormous desire of the people for ordinary lives and their understanding that ordinary lives are enabled by rule of law, predictability, and order. That is grounds for hope

I question the mental model and view, which may be informed by the 1980s and the 1990s in Afghanistan, of the country as ungovernable as a state of nature, of the warlordism that is so different from the tribal culture in the country.

The second ground for hope is that appropriate governance was absolutely possible in the country is the 1950s and 1960s, the middle years of the last century. Amin Tarzi is an absolute expert on this period. How was the state formed? And how did it function?

I recently received a 1950s manual from another Afghan expert, which is a picture book showing governance functioning in all the provinces in all the line ministries of industrial factories, of education departments, of health departments.

I think the third reason we really have grounds for hope is the period of 2001 to 2005, after the tragedy of 9/11, after the Bonn Agreement, where for the first three years, it was possible to establish institutions in Afghanistan. I had the enormous privilege to serve on the ground at that time and witnessed the establishment of the 1st Battalion of the Afghan National Army [ANA]. In just six months it went from an idea in a small group of people's minds to its graduation. Watching the pride of ordinary Afghan citizens and seeing that battalion march down the street was incredible.

The National Solidarity Program was rolled out. It gives a block grant to every village in the country where the village *shuras* elect their council, decide on their projects, and manage it themselves. It is now in 23,000 villages. This wasn't rocket science; it is a system that works.

The same with the health program, the same with the currency conversion and telecoms. Each of these programs required very few civilians, most were designed by a handful of people. And they were driven by committed and dedicated Afghan leadership.

I think good governance is possible. It is also necessary for Afghanistan to rejoin the community of nations as a responsible sovereign power, responsible both to its international obligations and its people. It will have to meet those responsibilities and manage its own institutions, and that is what is going to allow the eventual exit strategy. We may not want to talk about an exit strategy at the moment. But it is inevitable that at some point, there will be an exit strategy. And that strategy must be dependent on a framework of sovereignty.

Then comes the question of what standard. We are not trying to create Switzerland, but what are the standards? What are the services? What are the functions? I am going to point to just four pillars of these.

The absolute first is security, the Afghan National Security Forces, most critically the ANA, a police force, and intelligence services that carry out their appropriate functions, and are the right size for the country.

The second pillar of governance consists of mechanisms for decision making. Perhaps we need to look again at the suitability of a very centralized presidential system and consider what those mechanisms of governance, decision making, and accountability are. Even within the constructs of the existing constitution, it was an enormous gain to have that constitution. But that constitution allows for all sorts of subnational laws. And I think those are the spaces where we need to look at how governance is carried out.

The third pillar relates to public finance and accountability. We hear a lot about the corruption of the existing regime. We hear a lot from the population about their dissatisfaction with the corruption. I think we need to turn that around and think instead about how we build systems of accountability. And that means how revenue is collected. I believe the country could be collecting somewhere between $5 and $10 billion a year in revenue if it managed its mines, border posts, and agriculture and business revenues appropriately.

This also means a budget process, the central mechanism of governance in any country. We need to make the budget process Afghanistan's central mechanism. Then, look at expenditures, at how the payroll system works. Ask, how do civil servants get paid? How does procurement work?

The fourth pillar is basic services. Roughly speaking, at the village level, they are expecting very reasonable things. As we heard in the 2004 *loya jirga,*[1] district leader after district leader stood up, each wanting access to basic education, health, irrigation, roads, and water.

It is very difficult to hold elections in the middle of the war. Maybe it wasn't the right process, but we are where we are. When the group of people put together the Bonn Agreement in 2001, there were very strong voices in the room who said, "Please don't rush to elections in two-and-a-half years because if there aren't the underlying institutions to enable fair elections, then it is going to set the country back." I think their voices were quite prescient.

Certainly, we now see the Independent Election Commission and the Electoral Complaints Commission [ECC] have admitted significant flaws in the process. We need to understand that it is wrong for the U.S. leadership or the Afghan people to get the blame. We need an inquiry or lessons-learned process into what went wrong. Essentially, what happened is that one person chose to, and was allowed to, commit systematic fraud, and the UN [United Nations] team permitted that fraud, and didn't investigate at the time what happened.

Afghans for Civil Society wrote to the UN leadership two months before the election pointing out what was likely to happen. Those flaws weren't addressed. Going forward to salvage the concept of democracy and elections and to salvage the trust and reputation of the UN in the country, we need to learn lessons and consider what institutions are necessary to hold elections. There are going to be parliamentary elections next year. Do we need, for example, a census with biometric identity for the country? How does the voter registration get processed, get organized? We need logisticians to think through these steps.

The election process did have some benefits, not least the vibrant public debate among the Afghan citizens about their identity and about what they want for the future. So I don't think we should write it off as a failure. Given where we are now, I think there are three options for forming a government. The first would be a unity government of the two

---

[1] In Pashto, *loya jirga* means "grand council." A *loya jirga* is usually convened for such major events as selecting a king or ratifying a constitution.

challengers and perhaps other key figures who would bring together the political forces and govern for the next five years.

The second would be for the ECC to invalidate either a sufficient number of boxes; one of the candidates; or the process as a whole, which is an option within the electoral law. Then, perhaps, through the good offices of the UN, with somebody like Lakhdar Brahimi who has intense respect of the population and the political elite in Afghanistan, to form a transitional government that would be tasked as a caretaker to regain the trust of the population, exercise governance, and hold elections again after a period of time.

The third option would be that the incumbent President Karzai forms a new government, either his own or perhaps he enters into a new compact with the international community with clear lines of accountability and responsibility, and signs up to a "road map" with strict standards of governance.

In general, we all need to move away from a focus on an individual. If we look back in history to periods of successful transitions in countries around the world, it was never just an individual. It was a team and a system of governance that was critical. I think we need to invest—and the country needs to invest—in growing new leaders who can work in the cabinet positions, at the governor level, at the district level, and not just in government, but in business and civil society.

Leadership is absolutely possible in Afghanistan. I had the honor to travel to Peshawar just after the Bonn Agreement and interview heads of Afghan NGOs [nongovernmental organizations]. They built 2,000-strong organizations running health-care and education systems. I was impressed then, and I continue to be impressed, with their bravery and leadership abilities. There are thousands of people in the country who could lead, but they need to be supported and we need to focus on that issue.

Finally, looking at the question of governance, engagement is necessary. But we need to move away from a focus on the state and Kabul to take a much broader focus on the Afghan people. So the approach of COIN [counterinsurgency] to stabilization of Afghanistan is tremendously important and exactly the right approach. We need to look not just at the state, but the balance between governance, the market and job creation, and civil society and citizenship.

We need to understand that the use of force alone is not going to lead to stability. We need to look at the other mechanisms of governance, of economics, and civil-society building, that have to be both complementary and integral to a COIN campaign.

We understand that it is the pull factor of good governance and job creation that is going to draw people away from the insurgency and prevent them from signing up. And it recognizes the enormous desire for change of the Afghan population.

Amin Tarzi

I stand before you as a living specimen of the times that Robert Kaplan and Tom Ricks were in Kabul. Yes, there were times when things were a bit better. It wasn't perfect, but the system functioned. I think when you look back at 2001 with hindsight, somehow the entire experience of Afghanistan pre-1979, the Soviet invasion or pre-Taliban period, was just thrown out the window.

We started on a tabula rasa, a carte blanche, as if there was nothing in there. I think that may have been one of the greater mistakes, of not looking at institutions, at the experiences of these people and also forgetting that history that was with those people, because it was not just a history of war and being wounded physically, it was a history also of psychological trauma and how each saw the other. All this has to be woven into the tapestry of how we go forward.

If you look at COIN as an argument between two ideas for the Afghan people, it is whether the Afghan people want the idea that is presented by us—the Afghan government supported by all the governments, including our own and the institutions that are supported—or what is out there with insurgency. COIN is winning that argument, winning the people to our side. That is the whole thing about COIN because in the end, it is about the people. That is the consensus here. The question is how to do it.

If you look at and analyze the recent election, it has unfortunately helped the insurgency and not us. Why? Because it has shown again that the insurgents' rhetoric, their claim that this democracy is fake, that it doesn't mean anything, has been unfortunately amplified by events. It is more an echo of what happened in Iran in June of this year rather than something

that we, the Western world and the champions of democracy, could offer. So, we have a setback rather than a step forward.

Let's take that into account. Consider the issue of Lieutenant General David Barno's point about how to restore confidence and trust in the government of Afghanistan. And here I say government of Afghanistan, and I totally agree with Clare Lockhart: it is not the individual.

The other mistake we collectively made was putting all of our eggs in one basket. I am not criticizing Karzai here. It is the fact that he had come to understand that he is indispensable. We made him as if he was indispensable, and are paying for that mistake right now. He thought that without him, Afghanistan cannot exist.

How do we restore confidence in the government of the Islamic Republic of Afghanistan because without doing that—even if we have an ANA that is capable, even if we have the miracle of an Afghan National Party, which is right now in shambles—nothing matters if the government of Afghanistan is not seen as legitimate. As I noted, we have already taken a setback with this election. We now have to think over whatever time we have on how to restore confidence. And part of this is not connecting. Part of this is mindset.

When you look at Afghanistan—that is why I called out its full name: government of Islamic Republic of Afghanistan—we have to remember this is an Islamic country. Sometimes we forget that. The constitution of Afghanistan is a very Islamic constitution. What is the basis of governance in Islam? It is security and justice hand-in-hand. That is another element that was forgotten in Bonn. When you look at the distribution of areas of responsibility, we took the military, the Germans took the police, and so on. Justice was pretty much left alone. We are starting today.

Afghan justice is not what we think in Western terms. Sometimes, justice is what the Taliban brings. It may not be a justice that we like. A magazine reporter recently spoke at Marine Corps University about his time in Southern Ghazni Province. He said the Taliban didn't do anything. They just had a very crude security and justice system. Initially, that is all that matters. Of course, later on, as the society evolves, you want other things. We have heard that while there was security in Afghanistan, there was not a lot of electricity or other things that we regard as essentials of life.

So, let us first provide those two aspects, security and justice. As we build and expand on those, taking care of essentials and finally the nonessential "fun things," you get the people really on your side. Then, we don't have to be there. It will be a country that can stand on its own. That is the vision. I don't think it is a dream. But it is a vision that starts with their mindset rather than ours, with their blueprint rather than one we provide. I think we have to work on that confidence yesterday. At Parris Island that was the saying: you had to start yesterday. We have lost that time already, so we have to recoup the lost time beyond anything else kinetic we want to do on the ground.

I totally agree with Colonel Jeff Haynes that we have a lot of leverage over the Afghan government. But we do not use it. Using it does not mean abusing or belittling Afghan officials in public. It means pushing backdoor policies with direct consequences. We just heard that in Tagab Valley, the threat of withholding American or French support made things change. We need to do the same thing in Kabul.

Certain people in Kabul are literally getting away with murder. And they are still in power. One thing we cannot forget when we talk about leadership that whatever they do wrong, we have done wrong. We cannot divorce ourselves from their acts. When they commit injustices, when they bring people who have raped, killed, and maimed thousands of Afghans and bring them into the government, it reflects on us.

I am being very blunt because we have Marines and soldiers there who are dying. It is important to look at what we are doing. We have to have a policy that whoever comes in power—and it will most likely be a government of President Karzai—when he arrives, he comes with a very clear understanding that this is not business as usual, with very specific benchmarks. Some of them do not have to be public.

Our negotiation tactics and the Afghan understanding sometimes do not match. Another thing, we have to look at what's next. We made a mistake with this year's elections. We did not prepare for it. If we look back at 2004, 2005, we left things as they were. As the election came in, there was a scramble. We were hiring people left and right in this very town to go to Afghanistan.

We have set next year's two very important elections already. One is for parliament, and the second—district elections—is one that was never previously held. The campaign to make certain that next year's elections are beyond reproach should begin today. We have all spoken about Afghanistan as a decentralized country. There is a way to use that decentralization legally, not as what Afghan government officials sometimes tell us, that "you are building a tree and are cutting its branches." No.

We are implementing the Afghan constitution, which calls for district council elections not by the government but elected from the people. This legally empowers the district. I suggested to Colonel Julian D. Alford that we not use the word *tribe*; use the word *district*. A few districts become a tribe. We can work legally through the Afghan system without changing anything in the constitution.

This needs very good Information Operations, something that could be done through the radio systems. Afghanistan is still a very illiterate country, so radio is king. To get people's minds on the election and that we, the Coalition, are working to empower them and make their government accountable, is something that has to be done right now. If not, if next year's elections are botched again, we are not going to do well in this place.

Lastly, for the Afghan system of governance, we have to force their hands in specific areas because what is happening, in my view, is a bonus to the opposition and to our detriment and also that of the Afghan government. The rhetoric that comes out of Kabul today uses anti-American and anti-British sentiments as a means to play their political game. We cannot allow a government that we support to make statements like theirs. That should stop.

We have to look at the way our message comes across to Afghans. Unfortunately, it is not very clear. We need a unity of message specifically from the civilian side. The civilian message must come from one source and have no contradictions. Different centers of U.S. power cannot send different messages. The UN and other agencies further complicate matters with their messages, which are invariably different from each other. Mixed messages result in lost credibility.

Jeffrey Gedmin

As best I can tell, everything is a battle of the narrative. In families, it is the battle of the narrative. It domestic politics, it is the battle of narrative. In office politics, he who controls the narrative often defines the day.

As many of you know, this fall, 9 November precisely, is the twentieth anniversary of the fall of the Berlin Wall. If you look back to one country, East Germany, over the subsequent two decades you could make a number of observations, including that it has been very difficult for the country to attain self-sustaining economic growth.

For the better part of the last two decades, it has been plagued by pockets of relative poverty and, in some regions, exceptionally high levels of up to 30 percent unemployment. It is a country, despite immense advantages, that in too many instances had been plagued by xenophobia, right-wing radicalism, left-wing populism, and anti-Americanism. This was the part of Eastern Europe after the fall of communism that was going to be the immediate and relatively simple success case. After all, it benefited from West German largess. It had an educated population. It was ethnically, religiously, culturally, and linguistically homogeneous. By joining Germany in unification, it became a de facto or immediate member of NATO [North Atlantic Treaty Organization] and the European Union and as such, surrounded by democracies.

I tell you this not because East Germany has much in common with Afghanistan, although they are roughly the same size in population. They are really quite different, as you know. In the case of Afghanistan, it couldn't be more different—a society that is largely agrarian, illiterate, tribal, and culturally complex, and facing a vicious and violent insurgency.

But no matter what you think about Afghanistan, its elections, and the future of that country and its leadership, we as Americans have to be fantastically patient because East Germany with its many advantages is two decades down its road to joining the West. Is Afghanistan, even with the wisest policies and the most perfect execution, going to turn around in five, seven, ten, eleven, or even twelve years? I don't think it is going to happen.

There are two points that I would like to make. The first, which is so simple and elusive in Washington, DC, is that Americans desperately need very clear war aims. A number of the panelists today addressed this, as did Lieutenant General David Barno. Those war aims should be so clear, they should be clear as a bell, crystal clear. Then, from the U.S. political leadership, for domestic and international purposes, the aims should be repeated hourly, by the minute. I don't think it could possibly be over-communicated enough. Speaking for myself, the first war aim is very simple, and it is why we went to

Afghanistan in the first place. That is to guarantee that we have a minimally acceptable government there that closes the country to international terrorists so that al-Qaeda cannot again operate safe havens in Afghanistan.

The second is to have a government or succession or series of governments in that country that are broadly speaking—and I emphasize broadly speaking—forces for moderation, education, economic development, and human rights. My fear is that at this very crucial moment, we are getting bogged down and getting confused. We are entering into what one of the panelists referred to as a "crisis of confidence."

Everybody talks about clocks ticking. In preparation for today, I printed out a number of articles from newspapers such as the *New York Times*, *Washington Times*, *Washington Post*, and *Los Angeles Times*, among them. Every single article cites timetables, exit strategies, viable timeframes, target dates, and deadlines. Of course, few of them talk about success strategies. We have done this before and we have been there before.

First comes the success strategy and then the exit strategy. I think if you believe in this mission and its successful outcome, we all have reason to be concerned. If you look at the Right, there is talk of the hubris of the nation builders, Americans who want to do social engineering. As one leading FOX commentator said on my television in my hotel room this morning, "Afghanistan can't be a democracy." We know that. It is tribal.

Then on the Left, you have overreach with people talking about our mission there to be the eradication of poverty, the end of corruption. The *Los Angeles Times* ran a piece two weeks ago in which a professor, a distinguished one at that, argued that if we can't establish women's rights in Afghanistan, we should go home. I am for women's rights, by the way. But if that means by American standards, by standards of 2009, by standards of Southern California today, now, next year, I am doubtful.

I think that there is a considerable amount of middle ground between these two extremes as this debate becomes more polarized and we fall into false dichotomies. I think there is room for measures that are appropriate, consistent with our values, and realistic, and that support our national security objectives.

I am president of Radio Free Europe/Radio Liberty. Europe is free. Based in Prague, we do more than radio. We broadcast to twenty countries in twenty-eight languages and one of those countries is Afghanistan. We do the same kind of so-called surrogate broadcasting that we did during the Cold War. It is not propaganda. It is not messaging. It is not strategic communications.

It provides a country that doesn't have a free media, or a country where free and independent media is not fully established, mature, reliable, and accurate, and provides them information in their language in their own domestic terms. Amin Tarzi made this point. It is not always about us. Sometimes it is actually—and surprisingly—about them. We provide domestic news and information to Afghans throughout the country in all thirty-four provinces with 100 reporters on the ground broadcasting in Dari and Pashtu, principally in radio—it is a radio society—politics, social affairs, women's issues, health care, music, satire, and on and on.

What Robert Kaplan said was so apt. He travelled there thirty-five years ago and found a different Afghanistan. What we are doing is not imposing. What we are doing is not dictating. There is a constituency in Afghanistan for pluralism and tolerance. There is a very rich tradition. We in our work found, find, and are finding that sweet spot, if I may say. We are, despite the threats of the Taliban—they kidnap our reporters, threaten us, and the reporters' families. You know why? They don't want us off the air. They want equal time on the air. They want to participate. They understand the value of the information war, of the battle for hearts and minds.

Despite all that, we are called *Radio Azadi* locally. It means "Radio Liberty," and we are the single most popular radio station in all of Afghanistan, from Kabul to the provinces. I am sure some of you remember that movie, *Miracle on 34th Street*, where they prove the existence of Santa Claus with letters. In Kabul and Prague—and Amin Tarzi knows this better than me because he used to work for Radio Azadi— each week we get hundreds, literally hundreds, not dozens, but hundreds of letters from young and old, wealthy and poor, and educated and illiterate talking about the issues that you would care about, that would inspire you. It gives us hope that there is this middle ground between some sort of medieval terrorist empire and something we would love, but we won't get anytime soon—a perfect Jeffersonian democracy.

Let me close with an appeal. I think we need very clear war aims. I think we need very clear expectations about what we can and cannot achieve. And

I think we must be very realistic about what is happening on the ground. Again, as Robert Kaplan observed, we work with the material we have. Well, I have two concerns in the debate right now that, I think, are either being exaggerated or misused. It takes us full circle and has to do with the elections and the general topic of corruption. I am for fair and free elections, and I am against fraud, and I am against corruption. But realism dictates that we are working with what we have.

My concern is that these issues, while very important and impediments to progress, if we are not balanced and keep them in perspective, as a nation, we will be acting without sufficient maturity and farsightedness. The goals are bigger. This is a nation in deep transition, which will take decades for it and its people to resolve.

When you read and hear commentary from some quarters about the election fraud and the fraudulent government and corruption, it is in my view, an excuse to leave before we have accomplished what we want to accomplish.

Part VII
General Officer Leadership in Counterinsurgency

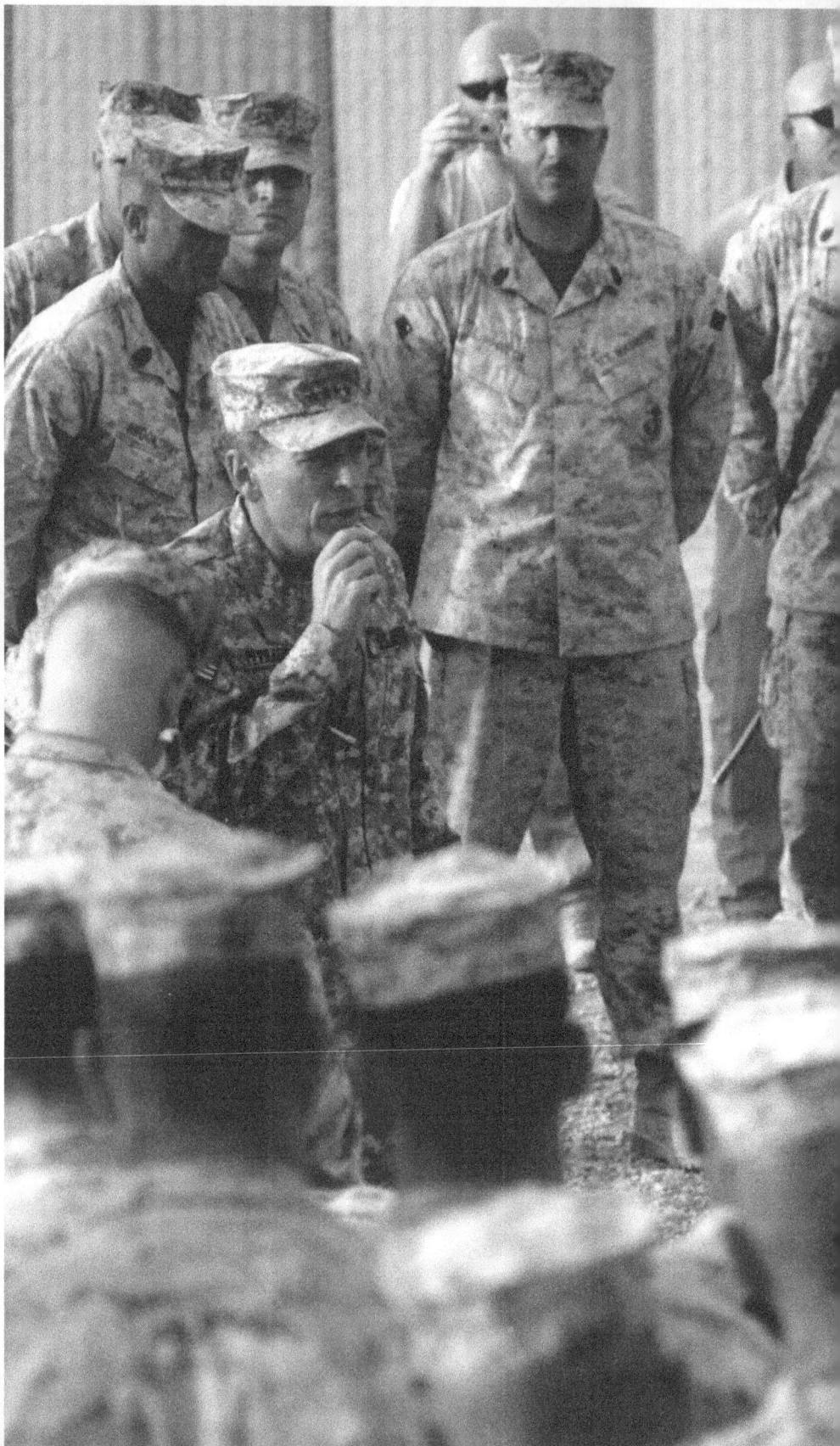

Chapter 13

A Conversation with General David H. Petraeus, USA

General Petraeus: It's wonderful to see so many familiar faces, so many important members of what's come to be known as "counterinsurgency nation" here today. But looking at a lot of those who are out in this audience and knowing that I've PowerPointed many of you within an inch of your intellectual lives on various occasions, I concluded that the most productive approach this afternoon might be indeed a conversation facilitated by a great Marine leader and a great military historian. That is, of course, [retired Lieutenant] General [Bernard E.] Trainor.

Well, that was my thinking, but then, being a U.S. Army general officer, the idea of a presentation without PowerPoint prompted me to reconsider. It's genetic.

And so what I thought I'd do is set the scene with four or five slides that provide context for the challenges that our leaders are facing in the overall [U.S.] Central Command [CENTCOM] area of responsibility and then have our conversation and Q&A with, of course, a full deck of slides available on call as required.

Finally, my apologies to those who showed up hoping to see this session be all Afghanistan, all the time, and to hear me divulge predecisional details on force recommendations or my advice to the secretary of defense and the president. As we were reminded, the conference focus is leadership in counterinsurgency. I know you've had some great sessions on that subject already today, and that should be the focus of the questions this afternoon. I can assure you it will be the focus of my answers.

I was privileged to serve one summer under the great General Jack Galvin when he was the commander-in-chief of U.S. Southern Command and we were engaged in El Salvador, Colombia, Peru, and a variety of other places. I remember watching him with the press and when he was done— I was a special assistant—he asked: "Well, what did you think?" I said, "Gosh, sir, it seemed super. You got all your points across, but it struck me that you didn't answer any of their questions." He said, "Well, they didn't ask any of mine."

This is Central Command [Figure 2]. Some of you will remember Central Command and a world prior to 1 October last year when there was one less geographic combatant commander and when Central Command still had the Horn of Africa. But with the standup of African Command that date, the start of the fiscal year, there are now six geographic combatant commands to go along with the four other combatant commands that have specified functions. Central Command is, therefore, the smallest of the geographic combatant commands, but regrettably, it seems to have the lion's share of the problems.

CENTCOM starts with Egypt in the west, Pakistan in the east, Kazakhstan and the other central Asian states in the north, and down through Yemen and the southern part of the Arabian Peninsula, the waters off Somalia—so we get to do piracy—and everything in between. All told, twenty countries. We have ambassadors in eighteen of them.

You can see the various challenges that exist there. It's a region of haves and have-nots: the richest per capita country in the world, and also among the poorest countries in the world, extraordinarily blessed in oil and natural gas, but often poor in freshwater. Some countries have spectacular construction activities ongoing, and others have very substandard services, inadequate

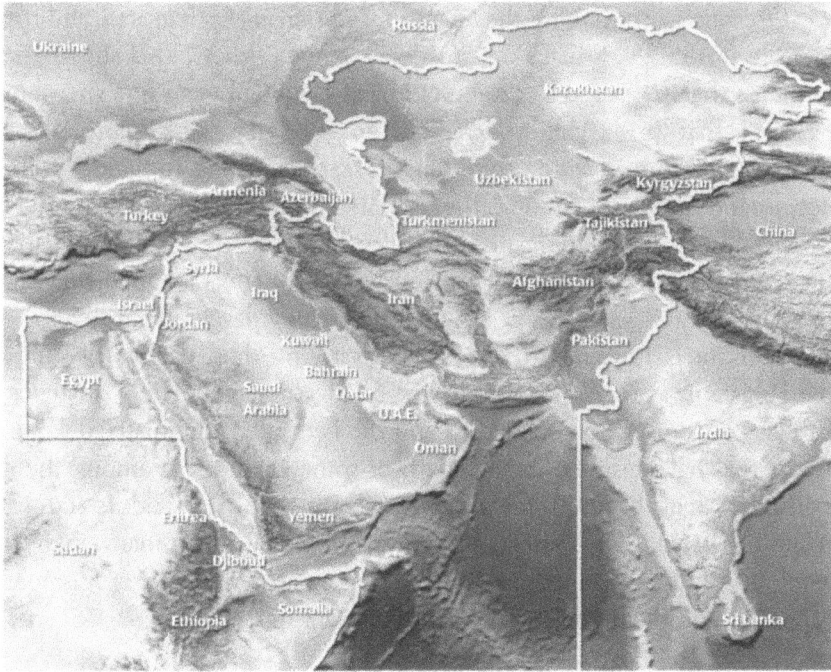

Figure 2. CENTCOM AREA OF RESPONSIBILITY

governance, and a host of other challenges to confront, and therefore, are, in many cases, fertile ground for planting the seeds of extremism.

So, these are the challenges that are out there and you know about them: al-Qaeda and a handful of other transnational terrorist and extremist organizations; we have the activities of countries like Iran which continue to arm, train, fund, and equip Shia extremist elements in Iraq to a modest degree; Afghanistan; Hamas and Gaza; and Lebanese Hezbollah in southern Lebanon.

There's the piracy issue. I'd be happy to talk about that. Touch wood, but we've actually made a bit of progress against that with the Zone Defense against the mother ships. They're parked off the coast of Somalia. The challenge there, of course, being a failed state. And, of course, we still do support operations that are conducted in this area by AFRICOM [U.S. Africa Command] with assets that come out of the Central Command region or from the naval component commander, Special Operations Command in particular.

Obviously, we still have the operations in Iraq, in Afghanistan, and the major effort ongoing in Pakistan as well, among others. This shows the elements that are in the Central Command [Figure 3], and in a snapshot what it is that we're trying to do across the AOR [Area of Responsibility] in terms of—to replace the traditional Great Game, the competition for power and influence among the powers of the world with a broad partnership against extremism in the illegal narcotics trafficking industry that comes out of Afghanistan. Obviously, a major effort is supporting our partners in Pakistan, where we've seen heartening developments over the course of the last five months, in particular against those elements seen by the Pakistanis as threatening their writ of government and very existence. But also in some of the operations and the Federally Administered Tribal Areas that have resulted in the death of some key leaders, among them Baitullah Mehsud. And there are the concerns about Iran and its actions, including its continued efforts in the nuclear arena, which many analysts would assess as the components of an effort to achieve a nuclear weapons capability and the means to deliver it with their missile testing.

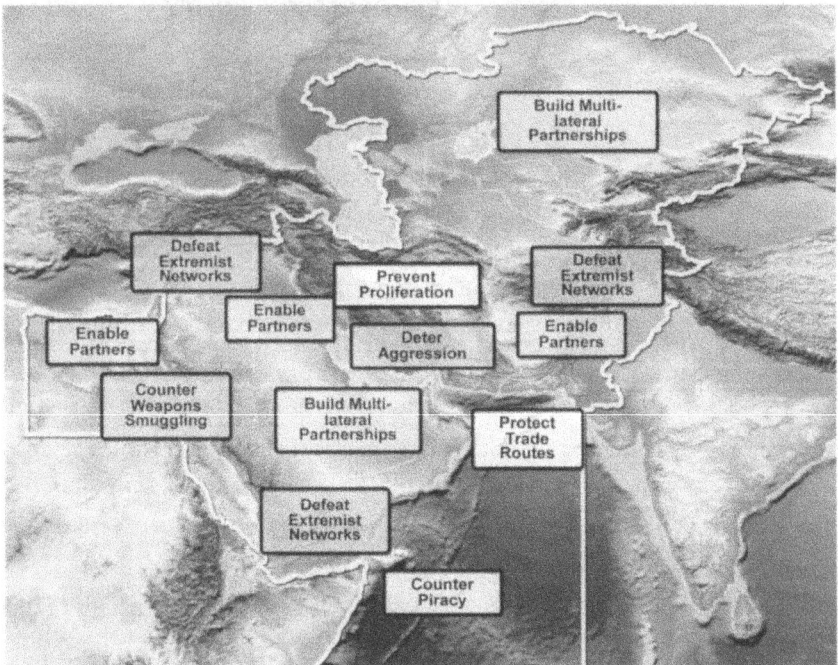

Figure 3. CENTCOM AREA OF RESPONSIBILITY AND FOCUS

I am happy to show you the latest statistics on Iraq where there continues to be very substantial progress, still down to somewhere around twenty attacks per day even with Iraqi data used, which we've now put in retroactively [Figure 4]. That's down, of course, from more than 160 attacks per day back around June 2007. Although we have seen horrific bombings back on the 19th of August—Black Wednesday, it's termed—by and large, significant damage was done to al-Qaeda in Iraq and other Sunni and Shia extremists still present. But there have been such vastly reduced levels of violence that the reconstruction has proceeded with the rebuilding of just about all the bridges that were blown up by the extremists back in 2006–07. And the pipelines are all flowing. Iraq has the highest oil exports in its history, and back in August the highest electricity production, I think, in their history as well. Plus the number of the major hospitals that are now opened—Fallujah, Basrah Children's Hospital, and others—is increasing.

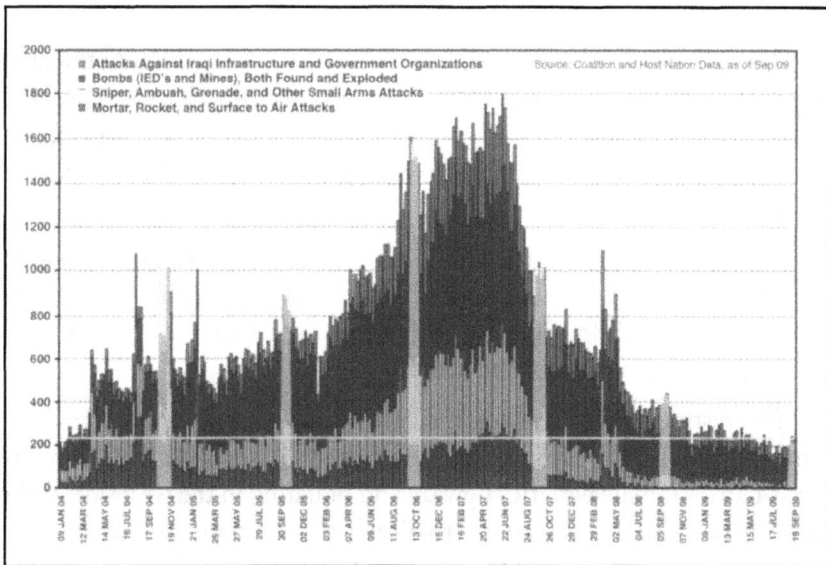

Figure 4. SECURITY INCIDENTS IN IRAQ

So there's quite a bit of progress there, albeit many, many challenges remain. The Sunni-Shia, the political "speed dating" that's going on as they prepare for the January 2010 elections—intra-Shia, intra-Sunni, Sunni-Kurd, or Arab-Kurd internal boundary disputes; you name it, there are plenty of challenges there and no shortage of issues that have to be resolved.

We continue to support the Lebanese Armed Forces. And there was a heartening development in the elections, not so heartening yet in the formation of a government by Saad Hariri. But they are coming along, working hard to continue the partnership, their long-standing partnership with Egypt. By the way, we're going to do the first big Bright Star exercise[1] this year that we've done in a number of years, I think probably since 2002 or so.

If you're going to characterize the overall effort against al-Qaeda and other transnational extremists in the region, I think you would say that it is mildly positive. Actually, the development extends all the way from the Federally Administered Tribal Areas over into Iraq; Lebanon; Egypt; the Gulf States; certainly Saudi Arabia, which has had a very impressive, whole-of-government effort to counter terrorism there—and there's something I'll highlight at the bottom here in a moment as the way of going after this—with the exception of Yemen, and that's where al-Qaeda in the Arabian Peninsula has established its headquarters.

This is a concern. Yemen is a country that faces the al-Houthi threat in the north, southern secessionists in the south, and they have al-Qaeda in the Arabian Peninsula and some of the southern tribal areas. So again, that is a concern and they do tie into al-Qaeda East Africa, which of course, recently lost its leader.

I mentioned the piracy effort and this very substantial series of partnerships that we have undertaken with countries along the western side of the Persian Gulf there, many of them in a sense motivated because of concern over Iran's rhetoric and actions.

Interestingly, Iran has been the best recruiter for Central Command when it comes to a variety of these activities. As an example, there are eight Patriot missile batteries now up and radiating in the west side of the Gulf in four different locations, two each in four countries where some time ago there were none of those. So a lot of other activities as you would imagine in the ballistic missile defense arena, assure early warning and air defense. Countries are very substantially embracing bilateral arrangements that we can then turn into multilateral effects, we believe with a lot of maritime activity as well.

---

[1] Operation Bright Star is a biennial, multinational exercise conducted by U.S., Egyptian, and Coalition forces.

Who is it out there doing all this? This was an insight out of the strategic assessment, and is not related to Afghanistan.

Let me very clear about this. This is something I've been briefing for about eight months since we had this strategic assessment by the great Colonel H. R. McMaster, who honchoed that as he did three of those for us in Iraq during the surge period in 2007–08.

The point here is that to counter terrorism—and I'm talking terrorism writ large, extremism—requires more than just your special mission unit forces. It really requires a whole-of-governments counterinsurgency approach. That does not mean that we have to be the ones providing the forces or all the resources or anything else. It does mean that many different governmental agencies, civil-military partnerships, and again, a comprehensive approach to these problems, is the answer.

I would hold out, frankly, as an example, what the kingdom of Saudi Arabia has done, because they have had a superb program. Yes, their assistant interior minister was nearly blown up the other day [28 August 2009], Prince Mohammed bin Naif, who has been a very important part in their effort. But by and large, the progress there has been very impressive given where they were four-and-a-half, five years ago when the U.S. Consulate in Jeddah was overrun, when their Ministry of Interior headquarters was blown up, when the oil complex was threatened, and when thousands of western workers were leaving because of concerns about the extremist threat.

The response that they had is actually quite similar to the whole-of-government approach that we used in the case of al-Qaeda in Iraq.

Now, just a reminder of the components and the elements that are out there: obviously, we've got the typical Army, Marine, Navy, and Air Force components, two of these full time out in the [Persian] Gulf, two that split their time between headquarters, although there are 70–80 percent out there. That's a little bit less than, of course, the four-star commands in Iraq and in Afghanistan. The U.S. Forces–Afghanistan is obviously dual-hatted as COMISAF [Commander of International Security Assistance Force]; then, two-star SOCCENT [Special Operations Command Central] commander. In addition to that, the two-star in Pakistan; two star, one star, one star in Saudi Arabia; and a number of other flag officers in other organizations out there because of the enormous ongoing security assistance efforts that are of considerable importance. I think they actually loom larger and larger as we try to build a network of networks as the regional security architecture, again helped to some degree by the concerns about Iran's activities.

Before we start the conversation, since it's about leadership, consider the metaphor—Mesopotamian stampede—for what we were trying to do in Iraq. The cattle in the drive are the tasks or the missions, and what you're trying to do is get them to Cheyenne, that completes that particular task or mission. But, boy, it's tough, and it's raining sideways. A thunderbolt might be an IED [improvised explosive device] going off. On the periphery of the herd, we're riding flat-out for glory, the handful of us that are outriders. We're all trying to keep the herd going. Some tasks—cattle—get out ahead of you and you'll catch up with those. Some will fall behind. If they're important, you go back and get them. The point always is that leaders in counterinsurgency have to be comfortable with a slight degree of discomfort, of chaos almost, of the Mesopotamian stampede.

It's a very complex endeavor often involving nonstandard tasks that many of us, for the first twenty-five years of our careers, spent relatively little time on. It's been an enormous adjustment. I know that you've heard a great deal about that from other speakers during the course of today. This is a great reminder of the kind of challenges that leaders face in what was initially, in particular, a fairly uncomfortable endeavor.

Bernard Trainor, Lieutenant General, U.S. Marine Corps (Retired): We went into Afghanistan to go after al-Qaeda. And we went into Iraq and AQI [al-Qaeda in Iraq] gave us fits for quite some time. You alluded to the fact that al-Qaeda is down in Somalia, and Yemen remains part of their nest also. How would you define al-Qaeda today, and how would you describe its state of health?

Petraeus: I think al-Qaeda is diminished over where it was, say, certainly several years ago. It is certainly diminished from where it was when we launched the surge in early 2007, again, without question. I think that if you look at what's been done to al-Qaeda in the Federally Administered Tribal Areas—and now I'm talking about al-Qaeda and transnational extremists in particular—there's been a diminution of their capabilities and assets.

That doesn't mean that we're not tracking various threats. You saw that there were some recent arrests made in the United States. It doesn't mean there are not alerts in some western European countries and careful tracking of individuals in various locations in that area as well. It doesn't mean there's not a link from al-Qaeda in the Arabia Peninsula to al-Qaeda in East Africa and then over to al-Qaeda in the Maghreb.

We can show and track the links within al-Qaeda. Now, showing and being able to target or disrupt or ultimately defeat some of those elements is another case. Often, again, that requires a bit more than just kinetic activity. It also requires, as in the case of Iraq, where you have to actually clear, hold, and build certain areas that were sanctuaries for al-Qaeda in Iraq, and some of the Sunni extremist allies.

I think that is an assessment that has been shared by heads of, certainly, the CIA [Central Intelligence Agency]. The past CIA director[2] gave a little reported, but major speech back in November-December last year that had a similar assessment, and I think the community's assessment is the same as well.

Unidentified: When the Obama administration did its original Afghanistan-Pakistan review, did you and the military provide the leadership and guidance of, "If you have the strategy, these are the resources you're going to need to fully implement it?" As you know, General [Charles C.] Krulak says, if you want to have a fully resourced COIN [counterinsurgency] strategy in Afghanistan, you're going to need hundreds of thousands of troops.

Petraeus: First, they don't all have to be our troops and there's a variety of ways that you can come at those. Everyone talks about twenty counterinsurgents per thousand and so forth. Those are in areas where you obviously have a serious insurgency problem. In fact, the density of attacks in Afghanistan is that more than two-thirds of the attacks occur in just about 10 percent of the districts [Figure 5].

So obviously, one of the approaches has to be to concentrate effort in those areas where the insurgency is most threatening the population and where you also have the most people and where they most matter.

Back in the process that was carried out, the so-called Riedel Report because it was led by Bruce Riedel—30-year CIA veteran, author of the great book on al-Qaeda, among other things—I did participate. So did the Joint Staff, so did a host of other folks.

---

[2] Gen Michael V. Hayden, USAF.

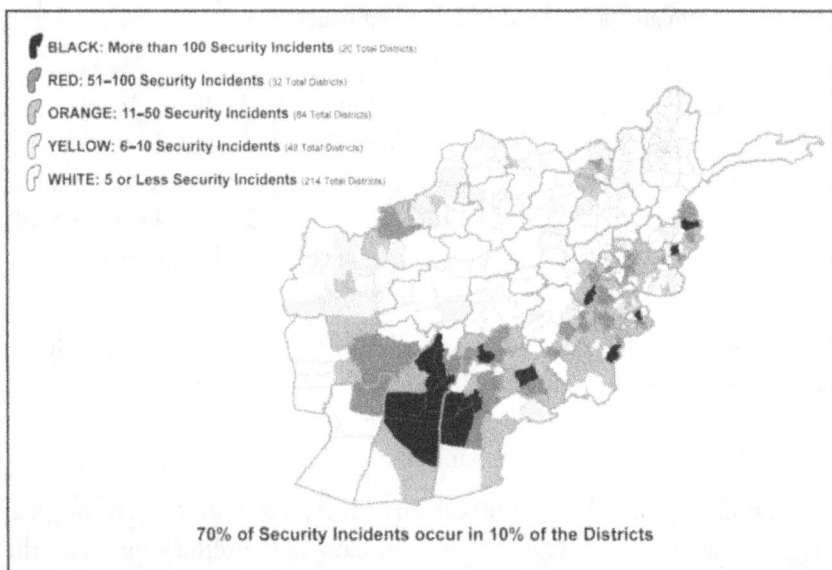

Figure 5. SECURITY INCIDENTS BY DISTRICT: MARCH–AUGUST 2009

This is where the insurgency is. These hotspots right here, and for what it's worth, when we did our operations in Iraq in 2007, we did similar density plots and focused on where the insurgency was. As folks like Tom Ricks and Linda Robinson remember, the first joint security stations [JSSs] that we established to live with the population was one of the big ideas: to secure the people, which you can only do by living with them. The first JSSs went into Amiriya and Dora, I think, and then Ghazalia quickly thereafter. They were the hottest of the hotspots in Baghdad at that time.

In overlaying where our forces have been going, we can show how the focus has been on Helmand Province and Kandahar, the original wellspring of the Taliban. You can see some emergence of problems out in Farah Province and Herat and then, a handful of other places in and around Regional Command East with a bit up in the Kunduz area as well. So again, that's where you've got to focus.

The president announced the strategy on the 27th of March. There are a number of documents that fed into that, in addition to the group that assembled to help craft the Riedel Report. I was one of those,

Ambassador Richard Holbrooke, Michèle Flournoy,[3] and then a whole team from the interagency and joint staff and a host of folks, many of whom I think are in this room.

But they also could draw on the so-called Lute Report that was done at the end of last year. There also was a joint staff assessment in Afghanistan and Pakistan. Then, in the study that was overseen by H. R. [McMaster], there was a component of the CENTCOM strategic assessment that also covered Afghanistan and Pakistan.

You may recall at the time we expected that there would be a form of assessment that would take place sometime in the fall. This may be a bit earlier perhaps than we expected, but we've had some events like an election, which, so far, does not appear that it is going to produce a government with greater legitimacy in the eyes of the people, although it's not done yet and we need to give the Election Complaints Commission, the IEC [Independent Election Commission] there, and others an opportunity to work their way through that.

And so, there's an assessment that has now come in as well that General [Stanley A.] McChrystal submitted here. I think the resource options piece will arrive in a few days as well.

But before that, we also had a civil-military planning conference. Ambassador Holbrooke and I chaired that here in Washington, brought all the players in from Afghanistan and Washington and those who were going to go out, Ambassador [Karl W.] Eikenberry, for example. In fact, General McChrystal was there as well. They have now produced a civil-military campaign plan that was one of the achievements of the month of July, the tactical directive that General McChrystal refined. It was originally done by General David McKiernan to reduce the level of civilian casualties—a hugely important effort.

You cannot have what appeared to be tactical successes actually be strategic setbacks because of the numbers of civilians killed. Those numbers have been dramatically reduced by the very rigorous implementation of that particular tactical directive, which provides guidance on the use of close air support and other indirect fires.

---

[3] Under Secretary of Defense for Policy of the United States.

He's also published a counterinsurgency guidance that is superb, something similar to what we did in Iraq, and even—believe it or not—a tactical driving directive. We were antagonizing the public with how we drove in Afghanistan. This is just one point in what General McChrystal talked about when he highlighted the need to change our culture, of how we operate so that it does not thrust the friendlies, the civilians, the neutrals, into the arms of the Taliban by the actions that we take.

It's instructive to show where our forces are because, with the density plots shown earlier, this is what we're doing [Figure 6]. As you know, the very first group of troops were ordered by the Bush administration and then the latter, 21,000 or so, by President Obama, taking us from somewhere around 30,000 to 31,000 overall at the beginning of the year to about 68,000 here when this is said and done. The additional enablers that were recently sent over there will take us up to about that number with boots on the ground.

The first element that went in was a brigade from the 10th Mountain Division in the Wardak Logar area, one of the hotspots that we had to contend with. We desperately needed helicopters, so a combat aviation brigade went in and it, together with a Marine Expeditionary Brigade, more than doubled the number of helicopters that are on the ground in Afghanistan. Some of the enablers, using the authorities of a combatant

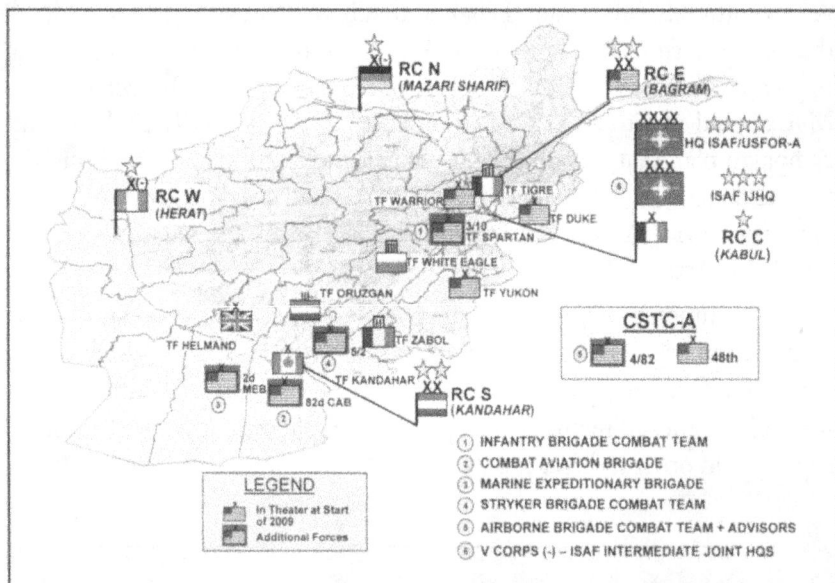

Figure 6. SECURITY INCIDENTS BY DISTRICT: MARCH–AUGUST 2009

commander, that were just shifted and been in the process of shifting from Iraq to Afghanistan will take that even a bit higher.

The Marine Expeditionary Brigade is, I think, the largest brigade in our history. It's got every enabler and everything else you could ever want. It is more than 10,000 strong and went into Helmand and has been working with the U.K. Task Force–Helmand there. There have been a number of high-profile operations there that have seen some tactical gains, and some are also operating in the Farah district of Herat Province.

The next element, the Stryker Brigade Combat Teams, was a very effective force in Iraq, as you will recall. In fact, they were so effective that we sought to keep two of them there at all times, and we were generally successful in doing that. One team has gone into Kandahar and areas around it, working very closely in that case with Task Force–Kandahar from Canada.

This is going to be very interesting to watch. It's a significant endeavor of using an advise-and-assist brigade, similar to the concept that we've developed for Iraq and are just starting to implement there. It is essentially a fourth brigade of the great 82nd Airborne Division augmented by a substantial number of commissioned and noncommissioned officer leaders above and beyond their authorization to enable them to do this advise-and-assist mission, and overlay, generally, platoon-size elements on the army and police elements in Regional Command South.

This will substantially address the deficit in advisors that had existed across the command. It will give a coherence to the effort—some sinews in terms of command-and-control, logistics, and access to enablers—and address issues that have sometimes plagued those elements. This will be very important to watch.

Then, of course, there are a number of efforts that we have undertaken designed to help achieve greater unity of effort. That's been another key theme of General McChrystal, but even before that, you'll recall that dual-hatted the COMISAF not long after I took over in Central Command. We had to do that.

We have also addressed a number of other issues. We compared the Afghanistan headquarters to the headquarters that we developed in Iraq over time, which was truly optimized for the conduct of counterinsurgency operations. It really was not much of a comparison.

One of the major elements, although there are many other smaller elements as well, is the creation of the so-called Intermediate Joint Headquarters. This is the headquarters that [Lieutenant] General [David] Rodriguez will command, the core element is the U.S. Army, but it is a NATO [North Atlantic Treaty Organization] headquarters, and it will be augmented very substantially by officers from all the different NATO nations.

A host of enablers has been sent in and others are still on the way. We still need, frankly, to see the effect that they'll achieve over time even as there is a quite healthy discussion about their efficacy that is ongoing with a considerable degree of intensity. There are several multihour meetings, for example, planned over the next two weeks with quite a significant time commitment by our most senior leadership.

John Terrett, Al Jazeera English Television: Could you kindly speak to the process of thinking through a change in strategy in Afghanistan from the counterinsurgency measures that we're taking now to the protecting of the Afghan people, to one which is more slanted toward a more distant approach, a more high-tech approach, and also brings in Afghanistan? I can't imagine who might ask you for your thoughts on that, but if they were to ask you, what was the thinking of the strategy that one would have to go through to get there?

Petraeus: That's another great attempt at an ambush, but to be truthful, that is something that gets into the very predecisional nature of what we're doing right now. And obviously I endorsed—the chairman endorsed—those who have been linked. I don't think [this includes] General McChrystal's assessment and description, but to be candid, that's not something that I feel that we could share here today. My apologies.

Marisa Porges, Council on Foreign Relations: We've been speaking all day about how to shift the focus so it's the training, leadership, and everything that's primarily oriented to be effective at COIN. But there are obviously a lot of other issues at play that aren't necessarily on the front page every day, but require attention. How does this wholesale shift in the focus of the Army, Marine Corps, and military affect our engagement strategies on these other issues and our ability to make headway on those problems?

Petraeus: We see them as very related. We tend to see, whatever the threat or challenge is, enormous connections throughout the entire area of responsibility. And we even, obviously, work across combatant command boundaries.

To give you an example, we run secure video teleconferences that may be co-hosted by the SOCOM [U.S. Special Operations Command] commander and myself, JSOC [Joint Special Operations Command] command, maybe General [Douglas] Lute, or someone in the White House, or John Brennan.[4] But they will consist of the entire arena that is out there. That is just one example. We see layers of layers of different tasks out there, but they all tend to reinforce one another.

So the regional security architecture may include substantial activities to develop centers of excellence, for example, such as the United Arab Emirates Gulf Air Warfare Center. For what it's worth, their sixty Block 70 F-16s are the most potent air force in the region, including that one to the east.

We have developed leaders who are capable of full-spectrum operations. We opened up the aperture. I can address the process that we went through in the Army to come to grips with this, and the other services did something that was very similar as well.

There was one huge idea. You know, we had big ideas before, and many of you have seen me brief the counterinsurgency big ideas about securing and serving the population, learning and adapting, fostering initiatives, supporting reconciliation, and all the rest. But we've also had the really, really big idea that all operations are some mix of offense, defense, and underlying stability and support operations. Frankly, that was a pretty substantial idea and we had not fully embraced it when we went into Iraq.

The truth is that when we asked for some of those stability and support enablers and other elements that were presumably available to help with certain tasks, when the brigade commanders and I turned to each other and said, "The good news is we own Najaf, the bad news is we own Najaf," they were not readily available, nor did we have the kind of mindset that was needed, but we were able to pretty rapidly develop over time.

FM 3-0[5] was huge. That was the really big idea. From that cascaded all of the others, counterinsurgency being just one campaign, or type of operation, along a spectrum of conflict [Figure 7]. After that big idea, we had to codify it in doctrine. There is a series of doctrinal manuals done

---

[4] Assistant to President Obama for Homeland Security and Terrorism.

[5] Field Manual (FM) 3-0 is the U.S. Army's *Operations* manual, published in February 2008.

during that time, including the manual on leadership, which again encompasses the kind of adaptive leaders that we're talking about.

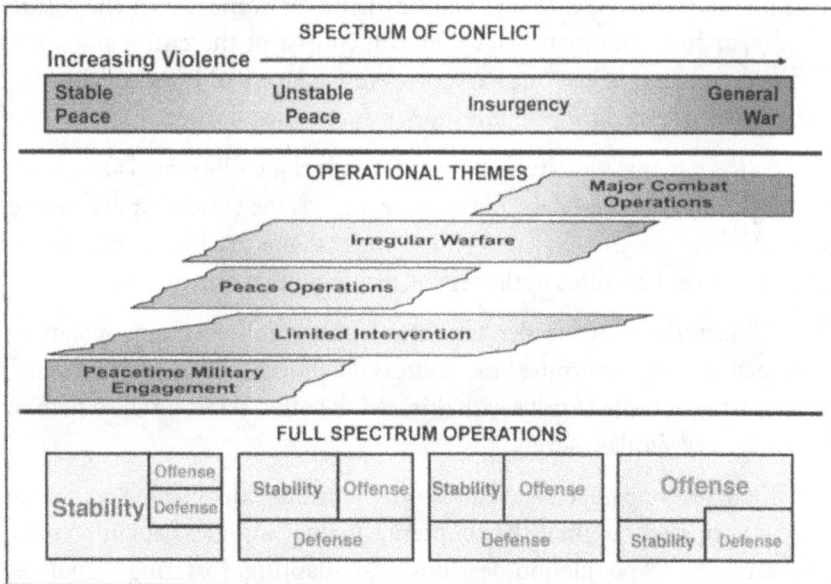

Figure 7. FM 3-0 *OPERATIONS*: FULL SPECTRUM OPERATIONS

Then you have to educate your leaders, which we did throughout every school and center in the entire U.S. Army. We completely overhauled these. There was one point at which the field artillery school commandant called and said, "Sir, just thought you'd like to know we closed down the field artillery officer advanced course two weeks ago." I said, "Well, great. Thanks for telling me. Good to hear it. Did you do it because you realized you needed to make some of those changes that the captains and we all were talking about, those guys who had been in Iraq?" And he said, "Yes. In fact we brought the captains in and had them help us redesign the course. They know more than in some cases the instructors did about what they actually needed to focus on."

I remember telling the Army chief of staff that afterwards. I sort of broke it to him and said, "Hey, sir, probably just so you don't hear it from somewhere else, we closed down the advanced course." He said, "Well, that's great. There's a couple of good things here. One is they did it. The second is they didn't ask permission, so this is good initiative. And the third is they didn't ask for any money or people."

So, you've got to change. We changed everything. We changed the combat training centers and where we do collective training from the "Clash of the Titans" out in the central quarter of the National Training Center. In the past we trained with pristine force-on-force kind of activities. Now we engage in complex counterinsurgency operations with hundreds of native speaking Iraqi or Afghan role-players. The Afghan scenarios have moved up into the mountains and a dozen villages or more look like Iraqi villages on the floor of the desert. The old activities are pretty much a thing of the past.

You next need a feedback mechanism, the lessons learned apparatus. In this case, the Service Center for Army Lessons Learned. Each service has one, plus there's a joint one. Those lessons are fed back to every one of the different elements so the big ideas can be refined, the curricula and seminars adjusted, scenarios refined at the Combat Training Centers, and change what you're doing down range as required. All of this is enabled by knowledge-management applications and virtual communities, which themselves are enabled by huge pipes that allow us to share information in real time, big data, and not have to do it in hard copy. The goal is to be a learning organization, and it is this right here that we're after.

The bottom element in every counterinsurgency guidance that we've published has always been "learn and adapt." Right above that, typically, is "exercise initiative." Coming back to where we started, a huge piece of this is the idea that you're not going to do just conventional military operations as we used to know them where you attack, seize the high ground, plant the flag, and go home to a victory parade. In fact, you're going to engage in something that will go back and forth from offense to defense, and will have a component of stability and support.

I think there's no better example of this, by the way, than the Battle of Sadr City when the great Colonel John Hort, after having the biggest armada of intelligence, surveillance, and reconnaissance assets in all different kinds of a really intense bit of fighting over the course of three or four weeks or so, defeats the militia that completely collapses. Within an eight-hour period his troops go from literally cheek-to-charging-handle to organizing the reconstruction of the area of Sadr City southwest to Phase Line Gold. That is an example of troopers who get it, who can pivot, and really do whatever it takes, whether it's very high intensity at low-level combat or very high-intensity stability and support operations.

That's probably getting at what you're asking about, although we obviously specialized to various degrees to ensure that we have people in the right places who understand our very arcane and usually difficult foreign military sales apparatus and security assistance procedures, and others who are also cultural and language experts.

There's a huge ongoing effort—one of the other big insights out of the strategic assessment that H. R. [McMaster] oversaw—that came out of the intelligence arena. We realized that we did not have the kind of capacity, the density, the sheer numbers of intelligence analysts and experts who could at local levels, tell us a very important data point: who is reconcilable and who is irreconcilable. The great Derek Harvey, who heads our Center for Excellence for Afghanistan and Pakistan at Central Command headquarters, spurred the program.

One of the huge components in the way ahead is that you've got to garner substantially more resources to push the Afghan National Security forces to a much higher number.

Another component that has not been pursued significantly or adequately so far is reintegration of reconcilables. It's termed *reintegration* in Afghanistan; in Iraq it was *reconciliation*. [British] Lieutenant General Graeme Lamb, who is now retired, helped us stand this up in Iraq as the deputy commander of MNF-I [Multi National Force–Iraq], together with General McChrystal, who was then the JSOC commander. Lamb, as a former director of the U.K.'s Special Forces, had a line into 22 Special Air Service Regiment. We didn't need deployment orders for their forces, so they sent us what we needed.

We stood up the first force strategic engagement cell and, over time, got the request-for-forces process going, and finally got them to institutionalize the concept. We were then able to intellectually develop the right and left limits and an azimuth that our leaders could then have something to hang on to as we sought to exploit the developments in Anbar province. This came to be known as the *Anbar Awakening* over time. It started in Ramadi around October 2006.

What we have now are leaders and troopers who get it, who are capable in a host of different environments and can fight, can do stability and support, and do all of that exceedingly well.

Austin Long, Columbia University: We've talked a lot today about building counterinsurgency leadership in Afghanistan and Iraq where we've had a robust presence. Could you talk a little bit about how we do that in parts of CENTCOM where you don't have that robust presence? I'm thinking of Pakistan, but also many of the other countries you mentioned.

Petraeus: That is a wonderful question because what I was trying to illustrate earlier is the idea that countering terrorism requires more than counterterrorist forces, it requires a whole-of-governments counterinsurgency mindset. It does not mean that those forces have to be yours. And I think Pakistan is a great example of that. There, the Pakistanis are doing the fighting for which we are providing substantial assistance. I think the numbers this year probably will be somewhere around perhaps $1.5 or more billion in a variety of forms of support, equipment, Coalition support funding, and the like. We're helping to do some training-the-trainer with superb Special Forces, and assisting in a variety of other areas, in addition to the efforts on the embassy side in the civil arena supporting a whole host of activities as well. But it's the Pakistanis who are out there on the front lines. Our assistance doesn't go below brigade level. And again, we are strictly in the mode of assisting where they want it. Most of this is in the equipment, but there is some training of trainers and unit training.

This is a case where we have relatively small numbers, but we're able to perform because we have functioning institutions. The Pakistani military is certainly a very robust and fully functioning institution with decades of development under its belt. This is unlike in Iraq where, after the dissolution of the military and all the other actions that were taken, we literally had to start from zero. There was not even a ministry of defense building much less a ministry of defense. We used the line that "we're building the world's largest aircraft while in flight, while being shot at, and while we're designing it," because that was the case. You had to get on with it. In particular, you had to start developing infantry battalions in substantial numbers, but at the same time you're trying to develop the ministry level and work it out so that the institutional elements would eventually mesh with what was coming up from below as you formed battalions, brigade headquarters, some division headquarters, and so on, to operational commands.

It's arguable, I think, that the Iraqi security forces have taken on the security tasks there. We are out of the cities with the exception of a handful of coordination centers in Basrah, Baghdad, and Mosul. Yes, there have been some horrific incidents, particularly on 19 August. But, by-and-large, Iraqi security forces have generally taken that on. So initially, we were having to do virtually all of it, and now it's a case where they are in the lead and, at most, we are enabling or assisting.

The operational tempo of their special operations forces has picked up; this is something that was hugely important and a concern in the early days after the 1 July change of us coming out of the cities.

Here's what you see, and you all are familiar with it. It started over in January 2004. Around the time the surge began, there were horrific levels of loss of life in December 2006—fifty-three per day in Baghdad—just in sectarian violence, and even more in some other categories, and we wondered why they couldn't get legislation. The level of violence went up when we began the surge of offensives. A lot of you in here who participated in that remember us having to fight to take away those sanctuaries to establish seventy-seven additional joint security stations just in the Multi National Division–Baghdad area alone.

After that the level of violence started to come down. There was also a militia taking a knee. That's the "March madness," as the troops called it, the March and April 2008 battle for Sadr City and Basrah.

But more recently, for about seven or eight months or more, you see a level of violence—when you talk about attacks this also includes attempted attacks, IEDs found and cleared—somewhere around twenty attacks or so a day. Obviously, a very substantial reduction from when there were more than 160 attacks per day on average in certain weeks in June 2007.

Iraqi forces have picked that up. Do we have a number of concerns? Absolutely. I mentioned some of them earlier. There is still al-Qaeda and other Sunni extremists, Shia elements, all of the political challenges and other issues, and still a lot of legislation that we'd like to see.

But you know, it more than stumbles forward. There's progress in a variety of areas. There's huge emotion about a lot of them, needless to say. Even the Sons of Iraq, by the way, have all been paid. They took two months back pay before Ramadan and have now picked up, I think, to a total of 5,500 or so just in the past month in integrating Sons of Iraq onto payrolls of elements in Baghdad. It's never easy. Every payday is emotional. It's all hard all the time. But, again, there is pretty substantial progress.

Contrast that with a situation where you ultimately have some forces and governance that's seen as reasonably legitimate in the eyes of the bulk of the population. Pakistan is, again, another case where we can enable them rather than us having to do it.

On the other hand, you see Afghanistan, where governmental institutions are still very nascent in some cases, challenged by corruption and a variety of other ills that Prime Minister Karzai and others are the first to recognize and admit. We'll again have to see how this goes forward.

Ann Marlowe, **Wall Street Journal** *and* **Weekly Standard:** I have a question about an unpopular group—the Afghan National Police. I would like to get your response to a radical idea: remove them from the districts. They're getting killed, I believe, at about a company rate per month. I've heard the argument that they belong in the towns, but where people are part of a homogenous tribe we would do better to rely on a tribal law, tribal collective responsibility.

Petraeus: Yes. Actually in fact, one of the things that is being looked at is the structure of the Afghan national security forces. It is no surprise that when a situation gets difficult in a local area, those who are most vulnerable right away are the local police because they live in the neighborhood. They are individuals. They're not units. They don't live on a base away from their families. Their families are vulnerable. They are very much in harm's way, and they tend to be the first element that will collapse.

We saw that repeatedly in Iraq. There were whole swaths in the country as we launched the surge of offensives in the "triangle of death" south of Baghdad and a number of other areas where there were virtually no Iraqi security forces whatsoever and certainly no functioning police. I think there were twenty in Yusufiyah when we tried to start recruiting and rebuilding.

We've requested several times—I personally have questioned and asked CSTC-A [Combined Security Transition Command–Afghanistan]—the training and equipping element, and General McChrystal has as well, to really look hard at the structure.

Everybody is always happy because of the Focused District Development program, but part of the reason that works is because you put the Afghan National Civil Order Police [ANCOP] in when you take the local police out for retraining. The ANCOP are units, essentially paramilitary gendarmerie units, that arrive in battalions. They're not from the neighborhood. They're not entangled by tribal loyalties. They have a base and can operate fairly freely without the kind of intimidation and vulnerability experienced by local police. And typically, they'll clean up the area for a while.

When you put the Afghan National Police back in, you have to have some elements there to back them up. Ultimately in Iraq, for example, we had to develop substantial SWAT [Special Weapons and Tactics] teams, Iraqi national police, and federal police after we reclaimed them from the grip of the militia in the spring, summer, and fall of 2007. To give you an idea of how challenging that particular effort was, the national police commander, both division commanders, nine brigade commanders, and 70 percent of the battalion commanders had to be replaced.

So I think we have to take a very hard look at the architecture of the Afghan national security forces. It may be that we have to do the same thing we did in Iraq, where the first element that goes in is an army unit. Once the area's been cleared, perhaps then you work with local tribes in some fashion.

There are some experiments with that, the Afghan Population Protection program, in the Wardak Logar area. There's another initiative that we're experimenting with, a civil defense at local levels. But they have to be tied back into something that has a link ultimately to the district and the province, and ultimately to the national. They can't become just tribal militias. So that is certainly something that folks are looking at.

The ANP [Afghan National Police], as you rightly noted, are being killed in substantial numbers. It's staggering to see the numbers. By the way, Iraqi security forces were typically losing their lives at a rate of at least three times to those of ours, many of those police because they are the most vulnerable. So you put your finger on a very good topic and it's one that is being looked at very, very hard, I can tell you.

Bob McMahon, Pennsylvania Veterans Museum: Many in the press compare Iraq and Afghanistan with Vietnam. Could you address how the shaping of your strategy and the lessons you learned about Vietnam maybe going back to West Point—not everything since West Point, but just the shaping of it?

Petraeus: I think people have been right to say that Iraq is not Vietnam. Afghanistan is not Vietnam. Each have their unique challenges. There are some similarities that you can always point to. In the case of Afghanistan, you have the sanctuary problem. You had a little bit of that in Iraq as well.

There are some similarities, but I think the biggest lesson of Vietnam is not to become a prisoner of lessons that you may have learned in a very visceral experience in the past. In my case, one of the challenges that I have and that many others have who have all now gone to Afghanistan—and we've assembled a real first-class team over there, we believe—is to make sure that we're not prisoners of our own experiences in Iraq and that we don't try to solve every problem in Afghanistan with the solution that worked in Iraq.

In fact, I've laid out at various times: here are the lessons that we learned, here's the counterinsurgency guidance that we employed and that worked in Iraq, but you have a real "buyer-beware" with that that says, "You have to apply this with extraordinary care and with real knowledge of the local circumstances in which you are applying those lessons."

Again, that's something that was lacking at the beginning when we did this strategic assessment. We did not have the depth and breadth and sheer number of experts on local circumstances. If you cannot determine who the irreconcilables are, if you can't figure out who the reconcilables are, it's awfully hard to foster the concept of reintegration of reconcilables, and it's awfully hard to separate the irreconcilables from the population so that you can indeed secure the population. So in that sense, I think what you really have to do is try to shed all of the baggage from the past, using it where you can. And there is the old saying that lessons of history can illuminate, but they can also obfuscate.

My dissertation was on the lessons of history and the lessons of Vietnam for the military, a lot having to do with the use of force and advice and the character of that. But obviously you can't do something like that without also looking at the kinds of lessons that we learned about trying to get the big ideas right for the time. I think that occasionally we shot behind the target. There are some real experts in counterinsurgency application in this room. And arguably, the Marines and a number of other elements at various times got it right, but then there would be other units that were still doing a big war or we might be doing counterinsurgency and they're coming at you with the big war.

You have to assess the character of what it is that you're doing in a very, very brutally forthright manner, very rigorous manner, so that you have—to use the good old Joint Staff term—a "granular" understanding of the situation at hand, and that's hugely important. I think that's probably the big lesson.

Dr. Peter R. Mansoor, Ohio State University/Colonel, U.S. Army (Retired): General, the one area of counterinsurgency leadership we've only touched on here today is civilian leadership. I won't ask you about anyone currently serving in government, but I'm wondering if you could touch on your relationship with Ambassador [Ryan C.] Crocker and with President Bush. What made them such effective leaders in a counterinsurgency environment during the surge period in 2007 and 2008.

Petraeus: First of all, Ryan Crocker was sent from central casting to be the ambassador of Iraq. I forget how many embassies he'd been the chief of mission for before, but I think it was six or so, and they were never garden spots. It was Syria when they overran his residence, and Pakistan right before. His reward for Pakistan was Iraq. He was in Lebanon in some pretty tough moments. He did have Kuwait at a reasonably decent time. He was the chargé d'affaires in Afghanistan in 2001, and as I recall, hoisted the flag. So he really was an expert in the culture. He'd actually served in Baghdad before.

He truly was a student of what we were doing and had been through this kind of stuff before. He was determined, as I was, that we were going to achieve unity of effort. You'll recall the civil-military campaign plan that we developed.

The first iteration of the plan was signed, I think, two days after he arrived and all we did was just the first eighteen pages. That's all you need to do. The leaders out there don't need a huge amount of guidance. If you say, "Secure the people and do it by living with the population," they got it, and they'll take and operationalize that.

Your job as a strategic leader is to get the big ideas right, communicate them to the breadth and depth of your organization, oversee their implementation—a lot of that by going out, walking on patrol but also through a whole host of campaign reviews, even the daily battle updates—and then capture the best practices and lessons.

On the second day, we'd already agreed the focus was going to be secure the population and live with the people. That was enough to solidify, frankly, what was already happening in terms of establishment of Joint Security Stations and some of the other ideas that were being implemented.

Cooperation was not optional. Crocker established that to the embassy. I established it to the military. We built fusion cells. There are limited numbers of experts in civilian agencies. At one point, we had to take down the deputy minister of health. So we're trying now to help the remaining deputy minister of health who's left and discover there is only one health attaché—one. This is for an entire ministry of health for a huge country.

We looked at some of our assets, and in light of a reduction in casualties, find we had a little bit of excess capacity. We asked her, "How would you like to be helped by several doctors, a handful of supervisory nurses, some hospital administrators, and medical logisticians and maybe a security force to go with all that and a handful of up-armored Humvees?" Needless to say, those augments were accepted, but she was the lead and was terrific.

We did the same thing with the energy fusion cell, the election fusion cell, and a number of others. So I think that is a model for what has to be done.

Secretary of Defense Robert Gates, the chairman of the Joint Chiefs, I, and others have all been on the Hill [Capitol Hill] saying we're the biggest champions of more spending for [the Department of] State. But there's a limit to how much you are going to develop, and the local population is not going to come as squads, platoons, and battalions with transportation ability to secure themselves, communication, and all the rest. So I think the partnerships that were developed in Iraq are being strengthened in Afghanistan because there is an increase in the civilian numbers there to go along with the substantial increase in military numbers.

Obviously there was a real focus on Iraq. There's no question that it was the main effort and we were pretty much able to build a team of first-rate folks. That's why I brought you back over there with me to be the exec,[6] and, you know, H. R. [McMaster], we were able to build on what was already a

---

[6] From February 2007 to May 2008, then-Colonel Mansoor was General Petraeus's executive officer in Iraq.

very good team. As folks rotated we also got some terrific people and were able to make sure they were all in the right place and to move forward.

More important, I think was building or helping the Iraqis build their team. I'm not certain how much you talked about that. Someone spoke earlier about replacement of various leaders, but the fact is that that government—you have to recognize that Prime Minister Maliki was selected—his strength was his weakness in the eyes of those who elected him. They did not want to elect a strong leader. They all wanted to elect someone they thought they could have their way with. And the fact of the matter was that he became very strong.

He became so strong that there was a point at which I came back and told Ambassador Crocker, "Hey, Ryan, good news is Prime Minister Maliki has just made a really tough decision. The bad news is he's made a really tough decision and forces are starting to move to Basrah tomorrow." But, by golly, that actually ended up being a tactical engagement that had a real strategic effect on the situation in Iraq and also solidified his position.

So again, there's just a lot of engagement, as you well recall, and I think that partnership there was something that rippled all the way down and to a degree rippled all the way up as well.

Colonel Larry Strobel, U.S. Army Peacekeeping and Stability Operations Institute: We've talked a lot today about being critical on military leadership. We do that very well and we get better because of that. How can our civilian organizations—whether they be interagency, national, international—improve their leadership to the current COIN operation so we can achieve success?

Petraeus: There was a period where the engine of change actually guided what we did in the Army [Figure 8]. The Combined Arms Center at Fort Leavenworth oversaw all the different gears on that particular engine. This included oversight of doctrine; education of commissioned, noncommissioned, and warrant officer leaders; scenarios of the combat training center for lessons learned; and even the battle command knowledge system, which enabled knowledge management.

There was an interagency conference that discussed how we develop greater counterinsurgency expertise in the rest of government, and we proposed an interagency engine of change. It starts with some big ideas and

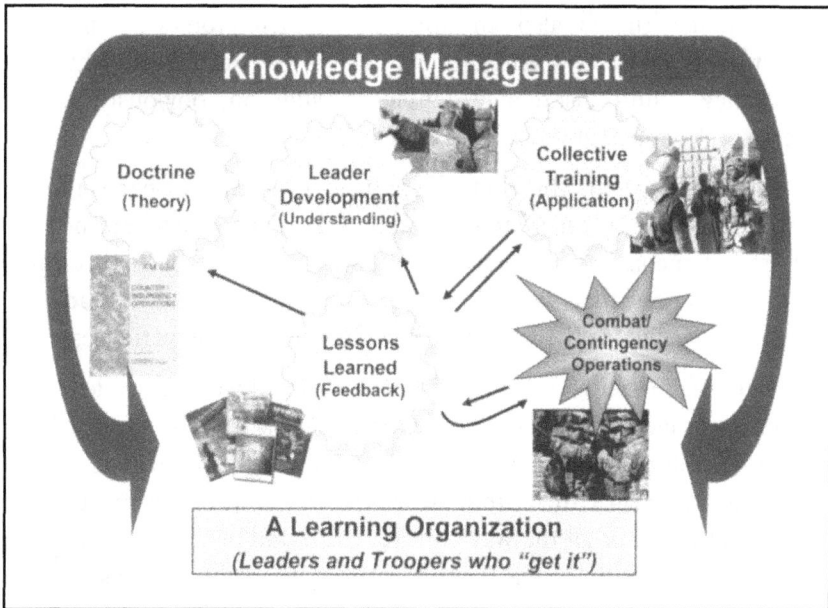

Figure 8. U.S. ARMY ENGINE OF CHANGE

then you've got provide the education. There is an education center at the State Department where they do counterinsurgency. [Ambassador] is that not true, that they have now instituted essentially counterinsurgency stability and support operations instructions out there?

Ambassador Ronald E. Neumann: Yes. It is slow. President [George W.] Bush authorized this stabilization and reconstruction force. It was essentially on life support until last year's budget, but is now hiring and moving. There are still a lot of pieces that are going to have to go. As you've had with some of your efforts, the length of time from idea to concept to full up, it is going to take a while. We've got new authorities. They're hiring— these numbers sound laughable to you but they're big to us—I think they're hiring either 1,200 or 1,300 state officers over attrition this year, where the last few years we didn't hire any. We're hiring at the bottom, our version of second lieutenants.

Petraeus: They can be strategic lieutenants, though, as you know.

Neumann: They could be strategic lieutenants, but they're not going to be O-3s and O-4s [captains and majors] for a while. There's a lot of movement but you won't feel a whole lot of effect for a while.

Petraeus: There's also an initiative at Arlington at your State Department Training Center there, which has also established an interagency counterinsurgency center. In addition, obviously, there's experience, but there also has to be education.

The challenge for the State Department has always been, if your numbers are never adequate to the overall tasks that are out there, how do you break someone out for one of these, out of their intellectual comfort zone experiences that we talk about? And I'm sure you've had that discussion here about the importance of those kinds of experiences.

It doesn't matter to me what it is. Grad school was it for a lot of us, where you go and realize that the huge debates you thought you were having at the staff college were in a spectrum about like this. Then you go to civilian grad school and realize there are some seriously bright people who are all the way out over here or all the way out over there, and by the way, they have some reasonable assumptions that undergird their intellectual positions.

So those intellectual, out-of-your-comfort-zone experiences are of enormous importance in the development of leaders who can take on these kinds of tasks. When you send a State Department official to one of our staff or war colleges, I think that's probably an out-of-their-intellectual-comfort-zone experience as well, but trying to break them free to do that—and I can affirm that, having gone to State and asked if they could send more people to some of the courses that we oversaw when I was at Fort Leavenworth—is the challenge.

Jerry Lynes, Director for Operational Plans and Joint Force Development for the Joint Chiefs of Staff (J-7): Sir, you know the U.S. government has put out a DoD [Department of Defense], State Department, and USAID [United States Agency for International Development] government guide for COIN. And I'm told U.S. Institute of Peace is going to put out doctrinal guidance for stabilization and reconstruction.

Petraeus: These are the big ideas that are hugely important. There were some others as well. There were some underpinnings already if you go all the way back to [President Bill Clinton's May 1997] PDD 56 [Managing Complex Contingency Operations] and some others.

Unknown: Sir, certainly you were one of the drivers of the engine of change for a number of years at [the U.S. Army Combined Arms Center] and as the principal customer of force development. The institution has come a long way in preparing its individuals and its units for the COIN fight. From your position, as the ultimate customer, as our principal joint warfighter right now, what needs to be done with more urgency? What emphasis needs to be changed? What have we not quite got right?

Petraeus: The fact is that there are a number of still very high-demand, low-density skill areas that we have to fix. So, there's a lot of structural pieces still.

For example, I sent a memo to the chiefs of staff of the Army and the Air Force and asked for help with developing more JTACs, Joint Tactical Area Controllers. There is a big shortage of those out there, especially as we now proliferate security teams out there in platoon sizes, and special forces teams need the JTACs from the conventional side of the house. There's a host of other examples of that in the electronic warfare and information operations fields.

Some real structural gaps still exist in areas that weren't all that mainstream or that important, or even if you had them on your books, you never filled the electronics warfare officer. That was the last person who ever shows up. If you really have 100 percent, then maybe you fill that particular billet. All of a sudden, when you're doing various serious forms of electronic warfare, that's very important.

There are big capabilities that are lacking. As you look at the whole cyber command issue, as you look at the issue of cyberspace—it's a battleground. It cannot be uncontested. The enemy cannot have free reign out in cyberspace any more than they can have free reign or a sanctuary in some physical geographic location.

Then, there are skill sets that we want to see more of in of our individuals, and that includes languages and obviously cultural expertise. Arguably, I think we built this in Iraq, but we built it the old-fashioned way, by sending people back again and again and again in substantial numbers. When you're in your third or fourth tour over there, you start to understand the nuances of it, even if you haven't really picked up the language yet. But you gain a real sense of how things operate, how systems are supposed to work, how they really work, and all the rest of that. We have to gain that in places like Afghanistan and Pakistan in much, much greater numbers.

So building that expertise, that's really also about the road to deployment. We also overhauled the road to deployment. Believe it or not, we were into—I think it was late 2005—I just asked, "Hey, how have we updated the seminar that we conduct at the beginning of the road to deployment?" It turned out that we were still teaching combat in cities that late in this exercise. So we said, "Stop. You're going to do a counterinsurgency seminar. We're going to start it next month. I don't care what shape it's in. It will be better than doing combat in cities." They said, "Great! Hooah!" We got after it and started that.

That kind of overhaul—you're constantly adjusting it—that's the real key, especially now as the Army becomes a lot more like the Marine Corps, Navy, and Air Force, where the brigade combat team is the centerpiece and you are almost treating those the way you treat aircraft battle groups or MEUs [Marine Expeditionary Units] as they're generated. That's another area on which we have to focus.

I do think that we have leaders who have demonstrated flexibility and adaptability. There are concerns at times, some of which I think are valid, that some of the technical expertise of some of our war fighting functions isn't what it used to be. For instance, we haven't massed battalions of artillery lately and we need to do some of that.

As we get the dwell time, for example, in the Army and in the Marine Corps in particular, some of these skills can be brought back. Then you focus during the final, say nine to twelve months of preparation on those skills that you actually need for the area to which you're going to go. As we've expanded, end strength and recruiting is going real well and retention is quite good. We've been able to build that up and start to implement that kind of program.

I was just talking to a brigade commander, for example, that the 101st Airborne Division is not deploying—not on the patch chart, as they say—for quite a while, and yet he has very substantial amount of strength of his forces, so he can really do the kind of stuff that was envisioned as the Army developed the force-generation model.

I come at it in terms of functions, tasks, and some expertise that we need to refine for the kinds of environments that we're going to. I think the key is this road to deployment, this preparation of forces, as we line them up against various locations and making sure they make sense. Recently we made a change and put the 173rd Airborne Brigade on the patch chart for Afghanistan, which is where it was last time, rather than Iraq, which is where it was slated to go. Another unit that had been in Iraq was scheduled for Afghanistan, but it's been reassigned to Iraq.

We've tried to facilitate this process as well as the Afghanistan-Pakistan Hands program. This program identified a substantial number of slots with critical expertise requirements in the headquarters and elements that support them in the two countries. We rotate the experts through these slots. The Center of Excellence at CENTCOM will be one of those as we go forward.

Contributors

Colonel Julian Dale Alford, USMC

Colonel Julian Dale Alford was commissioned as a second lieutenant in the Marine Corps in December 1987. He commanded a rifle platoon during Operation Just Cause and a mortar platoon during Operations Desert Shield and Desert Storm. In 1997, he received the Leftwich Trophy. Deploying to Afghanistan in May 2004 in support of Operation Enduring Freedom, he commanded the 3d Battalion, 6th Marine Regiment. In August 2005, he took this battalion to western Iraq. Colonel Alford attended the Amphibious Warfare School, and was a distinguished graduate at the Marine Corps Command and Staff College. After completing the Marine Corps War College in June 2007, he served on the faculty of the Marine Corps Command and Staff College. His next assignment was as a Joint Ground Operations Officer with the Institute for Defense Analyses in the Joint Advanced Warfighting Division. He is currently the commanding officer of The Basic School.

Lieutenant General David W. Barno, USA (Ret)

Lieutenant General David W. Barno, USA (Ret), was commissioned as an infantry officer from the United States Military Academy in 1976. He also holds a Master of Arts degree in national security studies from Georgetown University, and is a graduate of the U.S. Army Command and General Staff College and the U.S. Army War College. General Barno has served in a variety of command and staff positions in the continental United States and around the world. He has commanded at all levels from lieutenant to lieutenant general, in peacetime and combat operations. He served as overall U.S. and Coalition commander in Afghanistan from 2003–05. He commanded over 20,000 U.S. and Coalition forces as part of Operation Enduring Freedom, with responsibilities across Afghanistan, Pakistan, and portions of Uzbekistan and Tajikistan. From 2006 until 2010 he served as Director of the Near East South Asia Center for Strategic Studies at the National Defense University. He is currently a Senior Advisor and Senior Fellow at the Center for a New American Security.

Paula D. Broadwell

Paula D. Broadwell is a Research Associate at Harvard University's Center for Public Leadership. She previously served as the Deputy Director of the Fletcher School's Jebsen Center for Terrorism Studies. Ms. Broadwell has held military assignments in Asia, Europe, Africa, and the Middle East. She has served multiple tours with an FBI Joint Terrorism Task Force, the Defense Intelligence Agency, and U.S. Special Operations Command, and in other strategic and tactical positions in the Army. At present, Ms. Broadwell serves on the Executive Board of Women in International Security and contributes to the Project on National Security Reform "Leadership Development" working group. She has a BS from the United States Military Academy, as well as an MPA from Harvard and an MA in international security from the University of Denver. She recently completed Army Command and General Staff College, and is now a PhD candidate at the University of London. She is writing her dissertation on transformational military leadership.

James M. Caiella

James M. Caiella, an editor for Marine Corps University Press, earned his master's degree in communications from Syracuse University's Newhouse School of Public Communications in 1981. A photojournalist with 30 years newspaper and magazine experience, he was senior editor of *Proceedings* and *Naval History* magazines of the U.S. Naval Institute.

Dr. Eliot A. Cohen

Eliot Cohen is the Robert E. Osgood Professor of Strategic Studies at the Paul H. Nitze School of Advanced International Studies of the Johns Hopkins University, and founding Director of the Philip Merrill Center for Strategic Studies there. His books include *Supreme Command: Soldiers, Statesmen, and Leadership in Wartime* and (with John Gooch) *Military Misfortunes: The Anatomy of Failure in War*. He directed the U.S. Air Force's official study of the 1991 Gulf War, and has served on a variety of government advisory boards, including the Defense Policy Board. During 2007–09, he served as Counselor of the Department of State. He received a PhD in political science from Harvard University and was previously a professor at Harvard University and the U.S. Naval War College.

Brigadier General W. Blake Crowe, USMC

Brigadier General W. Blake Crowe is currently assigned as the Deputy Commander, United States Forces–Japan. General Crowe's military education includes Marine Corps Command and Staff College (nonresident) and CMC Fellowship at Rand Corporation. His command and staff positions include command of Kilo Company, 3d Battalion, 9th Marines, during Operations Desert Shield and Desert Storm; command of 1st Force Reconnaissance Company, Direct Action Platoon, during 13th Marine Expeditionary Unit (Special Operations Capable) deployment and Desert Storm ceasefire agreement; command of 3d Battalion, 4th Marines; AC/S G-3 Training and Education Command from July 2003 to June 2005; and command of 7th Marine Regiment, Twentynine Palms, California, from July 2005 to June 2007. He deployed to western al-Anbar, Iraq, as commander of Regimental Combat Team 7 from January 2006 to February 2007. From July 2007 to August 2008, he commanded Marine Barracks, Washington, DC. From August 2008 to June 2010, he served as Principal Director, Deputy Assistant Secretary of Defense for South and Southeast Asia, Office of the Secretary of Defense.

Nathaniel C. Fick

Nathaniel C. Fick is the Chief Executive Officer of the Center for a New American Security. Prior to joining the center, Fick served as a Marine Corps infantry officer, with combat tours in Afghanistan and Iraq. He served in 2007 as a civilian instructor at the Afghanistan Counterinsurgency Academy in Kabul. Mr. Fick is the author of the 2005 *New York Times* bestseller *One Bullet Away*, recognized as one of the "Best Books of the Year" by the *Washington Post*. He is a member of the Council on Foreign Relations and the International Institute for Strategic Studies, and serves on the boards of the Marine Corps Scholarship Foundation and the Rockefeller Center for Public Policy at Dartmouth College. He holds an AB degree with high honors in classics from Dartmouth, an MPA in international security policy from the Kennedy School of Government at Harvard, and an MBA from the Harvard Business School.

Colonel David J. Furness, USMC

Colonel David J. Furness currently serves as the commanding officer of the 1st Marine Regiment. His previous assignment was as Director, Marine Corps Legislative Liaison, U.S. House of Representatives at Headquarters Marine Corps, Office of Legislative Affairs. Colonel Furness's military education includes Marine Corps Command and Staff College (resident); the School of Advanced Warfighting; and graduation from the Naval War College. His command positions have included rifle platoon commander; 81mm mortar platoon commander; rifle company commander; commanding officer of Marine Corps Recruiting Station, Sacramento, California; and commanding officer of 1st Battalion, 1st Marines. From December 2004 to June 2005, he deployed to the United States Central Command Area of Responsibility as the commanding officer of Battalion Landing Team 1/1, the Ground Combat Element of the 15th Marine Expeditionary Unit (Special Operations Capable), and participated in Operation Unified Assistance and Operation Iraqi Freedom III in south Baghdad, Iraq. From 20 January to 18 August 2006, he deployed as Commanding Officer, Task Force 1/1, Regimental Combat Team 5, in support of Operation Iraqi Freedom 05-07.1, operating principally in the cities of Karmah and western Baghdad, Iraq.

Dr. Jeffrey Gedmin

Dr. Jeffrey Gedmin was named President and Chief Executive Officer of Radio Free Europe/Radio Liberty on 2 February 2007. Prior to this, Dr. Gedmin was Director of the Aspen Institute in Berlin, and before that, he was a Resident Scholar at the American Enterprise Institute in Washington, DC. He is the author of the book *The Hidden Hand: Gorbachev and the Collapse of East Germany* (1992). His articles on U.S. foreign policy and American public diplomacy have appeared in leading U.S. and European publications, including the *Financial Times, New York Times, Washington Post, Wall Street Journal, New Republic,* and *London Times.* Dr. Gedmin holds a PhD in German Area Studies and Linguistics from Georgetown University. He earned a master's degree in German area studies (literature concentration) and a BA in music from American University in Washington, DC.

Colonel Jeffrey M. Haynes, USMC

Colonel Jeffrey M. Haynes, USMC, is a graduate of the Amphibious Warfare School, Marine Corps Command and Staff College, and Air War College. In November 2007, Colonel Haynes assumed duties as Commanding Officer, Regional Corps Advisor Command 3-5 (RCAC 3-5), consisting of 150 Marines and sailors. In February 2008, RCAC 3-5 deployed to Afghanistan. Once in country, RCAC 3-5 expanded to include twenty-two Embedded Training Teams made up of 700 personnel from six contributing nations. These teams advised elements of the 201st Corps, Afghan National Army, during the planning and execution of combat operations in eastern Afghanistan. Colonel Haynes also functioned as the advisor to the Commanding General, 201st Corps. During 2008, 201st Corps conceived and executed a holistic counterinsurgency campaign in the Tagab valley, a longtime insurgent stronghold. He is currently Assistant Chief of Staff, Marine Forces Pacific.

Colonel William M. Jurney, USMC

Colonel William M. "Bill" Jurney enlisted in the Marine Corps as an active duty infantryman in 1987, earning his commission through the Enlisted Commissioning Program. He is currently Chief of Staff for Logistics at Marine Forces Command. Before assuming this position, he was assigned as the Chief, Plans and Future Operations Division, U.S. Joint Forces Command. He served as the Commanding Officer, 1st Battalion, 6th Marines, 2d Marine Division, deploying the battalion twice in support of Operation Iraqi Freedom—first in March 2005 to Fallujah, Iraq, and again in August 2006 to Ramadi, the capital city of al-Anbar Province. Other operational tours include service with the 22d MEU in support of Operation Sharp Edge, Monrovia, Liberia; Operations Desert Shield and Desert Storm; two independent company deployments to Port-au-Prince, Haiti, in support of Operation Uphold Democracy; a deployment with the 26th MEU in support of Operations Allied Force (Adriatic), Shining Hope (Albania), Joint Guardian Initial Entry Forces (Kosovo), and Avid Response (Turkey).

Robert D. Kaplan

Robert D. Kaplan is a Senior Fellow at the Center for a New American Security in Washington, DC, and a national correspondent for the *Atlantic*. He is the bestselling author of twelve books on international affairs and travel, which have been translated into many languages. His *Balkan Ghosts* was chosen by the *New York Times Book Review* as one of the "best books" of 1993, and by Amazon.com as one of the best travel books of all time. *The Arabists, The Ends of the Earth, An Empire Wilderness, Eastward to Tartary*, and *Warrior Politics* were all chosen by the *New York Times* as "notable" books of the year. The *Wall Street Journal* named *The Arabists* as one of the best five books written about America's historical involvement in the Middle East. Kaplan's essays have appeared on the editorial pages of the *New York Times, Wall Street Journal, Washington Post*, and *Los Angeles Times*.

Clare Lockhart

Clare Lockhart is cofounder and Director of the Institute for State Effectiveness, which focuses on enhancing the relationships between the state, global, and local financial markets and civil society in unstable states. The institute is currently working with a wide variety of governments and political leaders. Ms. Lockhart is the author of *Fixing Failed States* with Ashraf Ghani and has written widely in the press, including in the *Financial Times, Prospect, Europe's World, Spectator, Washington Post*, and *Slate*. She has also appeared on radio and television, including *Charlie Rose*, NPR, and the BBC's *Today* and *World Service*. From 2001 through 2005, Ms. Lockhart was United Nations Adviser to the Bonn Agreement in Afghanistan, then was seconded to the Afghan Government. Living in Kabul, she stewarded numerous governmental initiatives. Subsequently, she was called on to advise the North Atlantic Treaty Organization International Security Assistance Force on a range of processes. She has degrees from Oxford and Harvard.

Dr. Peter R. Mansoor, Colonel, USA (Ret)

Dr. Peter R. Mansoor, Colonel, USA (Ret), is the General Raymond E. Mason, Jr., Chair of Military History at Ohio State University. He assumed this position in September 2008 after a 26-year career in the U.S. Army that culminated in his service as the executive officer to General David Petraeus, the commanding general of Multi National Force–Iraq. Colonel Mansoor commanded the 1st Brigade, 1st Armored Division, in Iraq in 2003–04; was the founding Director of the U.S. Army/Marine Corps Counterinsurgency Center in 2006; and served on the Joint Chiefs of Staff "Council of Colonels" that reexamined the strategy for the Iraq War. Dr. Mansoor is the author of *Baghdad at Sunrise: A Brigade Commander's War in Iraq*, an account of his brigade's operations and the difficulties of the U.S. war in Iraq during the crucial first year of the conflict.

Brigadier General H. R. McMaster, USA

Brigadier General H. R. McMaster is currently the Deputy to the Commander for Planning at International Security Assistance Forces headquarters in Afghanistan. General McMaster's military education includes the Combined Arms and Services Staff School, Command and General Staff College, and a U.S. Army War College fellowship at the Hoover Institution. His command and staff positions include command of Eagle Troop, Second Squadron, during Operations Desert Shield and Desert Storm; command of the 1st Squadron, 4th Cavalry; Director, Commander's Advisory Group at U.S. Central Command from May 2003 to May 2004; command of the 3d Armored Cavalry Regiment at Fort Carson, Colorado (which included a one-year combat mission in Iraq); and Senior Research Associate at the International Institute for Strategic Studies in London from July 2006 until June 2008. During that time, he also served in Iraq as Special Assistant to Commander, Multi National Force–Iraq. From 2008 until 2010, he was Director of Concept Development and Experimentation at the Army Capabilities Integration Center.

Dr. Mark Moyar

Dr. Mark Moyar is currently Director of Research at Orbis Operations. Before accepting this position, he was Professor of National Security Affairs at the Marine Corps University, where he taught at its component schools, including the Command and Staff College and the War College. His most recent book is *A Question of Command: Counterinsurgency from the Civil War to Iraq*, published in September 2009. He has also written two books on the Vietnam War: *Triumph Forsaken: The Vietnam War, 1954–1965* and *Phoenix and the Birds of Prey: Counterinsurgency and Counterterrorism in Vietnam. Triumph Forsaken* is one of the most-discussed histories of the past decade and has been the subject of an academic conference and the book *Triumph Revisited: Historians Battle for the Vietnam War* (2010). Dr. Moyar's writings have appeared in the *New York Times, Washington Post, Wall Street Journal*, and many other publications. He received a BA summa cum laude from Harvard and a PhD from Cambridge.

Major General Robert B. Neller, USMC

Major General Robert B. Neller was commissioned as a Marine officer through the Platoon Leaders Class program in May 1975. He is a graduate of the Marine Corps Command and Staff College, the Armed Forces Staff College, and the NATO Defense College, and has participated in a wide variety of military operations. As Commanding Officer, Marine Corps Security Force Company, Panama, he participated in Operations Just Cause and Promote Liberty. He commanded the 3d Light Armored Infantry Battalion and deployed to Somalia in support of Operation Restore Hope. In September 2005, he was assigned as the Deputy Commanding General (Operations), I Marine Expeditionary Force (Forward), and deployed to Iraq in support of Operation Iraqi Freedom from February 2006 to February 2007. Major General Neller served as Commanding General, 3d Marine Division, from June 2007 to August 2009 and transitioned to President, Marine Corps University, and Commanding General, Education Command, on 4 September 2009. In December 2010, he was promoted to lieutenant general and assumed duties as Director of Operations, Joint Staff.

General David H. Petraeus, USA

General David H. Petraeus is a graduate of the United States Military Academy and the U.S. Army Command and General Staff College. After earning MPA and PhD degrees in International Relations from Princeton University, he served as an Assistant Professor of International Relations at the U.S. Military Academy. General Petraeus has held leadership positions in airborne, mechanized, and air assault infantry units in Europe and the United States. In 2003, he commanded the 101st Airborne Division (Air Assault) for the first year of Operation Iraqi Freedom. General Petraeus then became the first commander of the Multi National Security Transition Command–Iraq. Returning to Fort Leavenworth in 2005, he commanded the U.S. Army Combined Arms Center. At the beginning of 2007, he returned to Iraq as the Commanding General, Multi National Force–Iraq, and remained in that position until assuming command of the United States Central Command in October 2008. On 4 July 2010, he assumed command of the North Atlantic Treaty Organization International Security Assistance Force and U.S. Forces–Afghanistan.

Thomas E. Ricks

Thomas E. Ricks is the author of *Fiasco: The American Military Adventure in Iraq*, which was a number one *New York Times* bestseller and a finalist for the Pulitzer Prize in 2007. His second book on that war, *The Gamble: General David Petraeus and the American Military Adventure in Iraq, 2006–2008*, was published in February 2009, and also became a *New York Times* bestseller. His previous book, *Making the Corps*, won the *Washington Monthly's* "Political Book of the Year" award. A correspondent for many years at the *Wall Street Journal* and *Washington Post*, he has been a member of two Pulitzer Prize–winning reporting teams. He currently is a Fellow at the Center for a New American Security and a contributing editor at *Foreign Policy* magazine, for which he writes the blog *The Best Defense*. He grew up in New York and Afghanistan, and graduated magna cum laude from Yale in 1977.

Dr. Nicholas J. Schlosser

Nicholas J. Schlosser earned his doctorate in history from the University of Maryland in 2008, and has worked as a historian with the Marine Corps History Division since 2009. His research examines the U.S. Marine Corps during Operation Iraqi Freedom, as well as the Marine Corps' involvement in irregular warfare and counterinsurgencies. He is the editor of the volume *U.S. Marines in Iraq, 2004–2008: Anthology and Annotated Bibliography.*

Dr. Amin Tarzi

Dr. Amin Tarzi is the Director of Middle East Studies at Marine Corps University. Prior to this, Dr. Tarzi covered Afghanistan and Pakistan for Radio Free Europe/Radio Liberty's Regional Analysis team. Dr. Tarzi has also taught at the Center for Advanced Defense Studies and worked at the Center for Nonproliferation Studies, the Saudi Arabian Mission at the United Nations, and the Emirates Center for Strategic Studies and Research. Dr. Tarzi is the author of numerous book chapters, articles, and commentaries on Afghanistan and the Middle East, and appears regularly on radio and television. He earned his PhD and MA degrees from the Department of Middle East Studies at New York University. His latest works are *Taliban and the Crisis in Afghanistan*, co-edited with Robert D. Crews (Harvard University Press, 2008), and *The Iranian Puzzle Piece: Understanding Iran in the Global Context* (Marine Corps University Press, 2009).

Francis J. "Bing" West

Francis J. "Bing" West served as Assistant Secretary of Defense for International Security Affairs in the Reagan administration. A graduate of Georgetown and Princeton Universities, he served in Marine infantry units in Vietnam. Based on his experiences in Vietnam, he produced two books: *Small Unit Action in Vietnam* and *The Village*. A frequent visitor to Iraq and Afghanistan, he has written three books on Iraq, most recently, *The Strongest Tribe: War, Politics, and the Endgame in Iraq*. His books have won the Marine Corps Heritage Prize and the Colby Award for Military History, and have appeared on the U.S. Marine Corps Commandant's Reading List. West is a correspondent for the *Atlantic* and appears regularly on the *NewsHour* and *Fox News*. He has also been Vice President of the Hudson Institute, Dean of Research at the Naval War College, and an analyst at the Rand Corporation.

Colonel John K. Wood, USA (Ret.)

Colonel John K. Wood, USA (Ret.), is a member of the faculty and was formerly the Director for Afghanistan and Pakistan Coordination at the Near East South Asia Center for Strategic Studies. Prior to joining the center, he served as the Senior Director for Afghanistan for the National Security Council under both the George W. Bush and Obama administrations. He retired as a colonel after serving 28 years in the United States Army. He served in the Pentagon as the Assistant Deputy Director for Politico-Military Affairs–Asia on the Joint Staff, and his previous military assignments included both command and staff billets in Korea, Europe, and the United States. From 2002 to 2003 he was the Military Assistant to the Acting Secretary of the Army. He holds a bachelor's degree from the U.S. Military Academy, as well as masters' degrees from the Naval Postgraduate School and the Industrial College of the Armed Forces at National Defense University. He is a graduate of the Combined Arms and Services Staff School and the Command and General Staff College.

Appendix
Acronyms and Abbreviations

AFRICOM	U.S. Africa Command
ANA	Afghan National Army
ANCOP	Afghan National Civil Order Police
ANP	Afghan National Police
AO	Area of Operations
AOR	Area of Responsibility
AQI	al-Qaeda in Iraq
BBC	British Broadcasting Corporation
CENTCOM	U.S. Central Command
CIA	Central Intelligence Agency
CNN	Cable News Network
COIN	counterinsurgency
COMISAF	Commander of International Security Assistance Force
CSTC-A	Combined Security Transition Command–Afghanistan
DC	direct commission
DoD	U.S. Department of Defense
ECC	Electoral Complaints Commission
EPRT	Embedded Provincial Reconstruction Team
ETT	Embedded Training Team
FOB	forward operating base
GAO	U.S. Government Accountability Office
H and S	Headquarters and Service

IEC	Independent Election Commission
IED	improvised explosive device
ISAF	International Security Assistance Force
JAG	Judge Advocate General
JSOC	Joint Special Operations Command
JSS	joint security station
MEF	Marine Expeditionary Force
MEU	Marine Expeditionary Unit
MNFI	Multi National Force–Iraq
MRAP	mine resistant ambush protected vehicle
NATO	North Atlantic Treaty Organization
NCO	noncommissioned officer
NGO	nongovernmental organization
OCS	Officer Candidate School
OEMA	Office of Economic and Manpower Analysis
OP	observation post
PFC	private first class
PME	professional military education
PRT	Provincial Reconstruction Team
PsyOps	Psychological Operations
RC	Regional Command
RCT	regimental combat team
ROE	rules of engagement
ROTC	Reserve Officer Training Corps
RPG	rocket-propelled grenade

SIGACTS	significant acts
SOCCENT	Special Operations Command Central
SOCCOM	U.S. Special Operations Command
SOF	Special Operations Forces
SSI	Strategic Studies Institute
SWAT	Special Weapons and Tactics
TBS	The Basic School
UN	United Nations
UNAMA	United Nations Assistance Mission in Afghanistan
USAID	United States Agency for International Development
USMA	United States Military Academy
XO	executive officer

Index

www.ingramcontent.com/pod-product-compliance
Lightning Source LLC
Chambersburg PA
CBHW060756100426
42813CB00004B/842